HOW TO GET RESEARCH PUBLISHED IN JOURNALS

This book is dedicated with love and thanks to the four people who have taught me the most important things in my life: my parents, Gwen and Stockwell Day; my children, Jake and Alexandra.

How to get research published in journals

Abby Day

Gower

Published by
Gower Publishing Limited
Gower House
Croft Road
Aldershot
Hampshire GU11 3HR
England

Gower
Old Post Road
Brookfield
Vermount 05036
USA

Reprinted 2000

Abby Day has asserted her right under the Copyright, Designs and Patents Act 1988 to be identified as the author of this work.

British Library Cataloguing in Publication Data
Day, Abby
   How to get research published in journals
   1. Research – Periodicals – Publishing 2. Periodicals,
   Publishing of
   I. Title
   001.4´05

Library of Congress Cataloguing-in-Publication Data
Day, Abby, 1956–
      How to get research published in journals / Abby Day.
      p.   cm.
      Includes index.
      ISBN 0-566-07886-4. – ISBN 0-566-07767-1 (pbk.)
   1. Authorship–Marketing.   2. Report writing.   3. Research.
   I. Title.
   PN161.D39   1996
   808´.02–dc20   96-21609
                                                       CIP

ISBN 0 566 07767 1 Paperback
ISBN 0 566 07886 4 Hardback

Typeset in Palatino by Manton Typesetters, 5–7 Eastfield Road, Louth, Lincolnshire, LN11 7AJ, UK and printed in the United Kingdom at the University Press, Cambridge.

Contents

List of figures

Preface

This book is for people who want and need to be published in academic journals – researchers, students and members of faculty. The pressure to publish is increasing as funding bodies demand greater proof of quality research and its dissemination.

Publishing may seem like a difficult and mysterious business, but it's not. Once you understand how to go about it, and what will determine your success, it becomes a deeply satisfying experience for the author and ultimately for the reader. This book is based on original research into what quality standards editors and reviewers are seeking and the combined experience of many authors, editors and reviewers. The conclusions they share are widely tested in practice in many different academic disciplines in many different countries. You can therefore be assured that you will be able to apply their advice with confidence.

The book is in three main parts, reflecting the stages authors go through as they work towards successful publication. Part I will help you define your objectives, allowing you to focus on the task ahead with clarity and economy. Part II invites you to understand more deeply the needs of editors, reviewers and readers so that you can align your objectives with theirs. Part III allows you to pull together all you have learned into a publishable paper. Each chapter ends with action points to help you apply the principles discussed and practise the techniques described.

I urge you to adopt the step-by-step process in its chronological order. The reason many aspiring authors fail is that they throw themselves immediately into the activity of writing without realising that it is the forethought, analysis and preparation that determine the quality of the finished product. If you follow the advice you will find the process of writing an academic paper interesting and pleasurable. If you adopt the approach recommended here you can easily write publishable papers in much less time than you ever thought possible. Most importantly, it will be a rewarding activity benefiting you, your institution, and all those who stand to gain from reading your work.

Abby Day

Acknowledgements

Don't you hate those speeches at the Academy Awards when the Best Supporting Actor thanks the director, producer, agent, lighting technician, his granny and his cat? Sorry, but this is the part when I do the same thing!

Writing a book, or indeed an article, is normally something of a shared enterprise. Writing a book about becoming published was especially so. Since I began writing articles and books twenty years ago I have been advised throughout by colleagues, editors, reviewers and readers. Their comments, criticism and encouragement have sustained and enriched me. In more recent years when I have edited and published academic journals I have had the great privilege of working with dedicated editors, reviewers and authors from around the world. To them, I owe most of the professional expertise I can claim, and from any of the more preposterous statements or errors I make they are completely absolved. To the many, many faceless beings on the Internet, editorial advisers and publishers who contributed, my thanks.

The first phase of my research on quality variables referred to extensively in this book was sponsored by MCB University Press. I am grateful not only for their funding but for the open access they allowed to their customers and staff. In particular, I thank, on behalf of many authors, Dr Gordon Wills, whose vision for worldwide authors' workshops and support materials demonstrate the value-adding role publishers can perform.

To editors and fellow authors around the world, who shared their visions of publishing with me while I was writing this book, my thanks. Many of their insights, including direct quotations, are included in the following pages. Several whose thoughts have been drawn upon more extensively include Dr David Bennett, Dr David Carson, Dr Maxine Clarke, Dr Rod Davies, Dr Harry Dickinson, Dr Steven Drew, Dr Stan Glaser, Dr Christian Grönroos, Dr Mike Halliday, Dr Margaret Redfern, Dr Bill Richardson, Dr Jim Stock, Dr Richard Teare and Dr Kathryn Todd.

To my colleagues at our publishing consultancy business, Red Swan Ltd, and in particular Dr John Peters and Richard Rowe, my thanks too. Besides being an editor whose careful guidance has earned him the respect of authors worldwide, John also has the mixed fortune of being married to me. His continuous professional and personal support deserves my greatest debt.

And finally, to my editor Malcolm Stern at Gower, for his guidance and enthusiasm, my thanks.

It's customary at this point for authors to say that they neglected their families and friends, went without sleep and created chaos and disruption whilst they were immersed in their masterpiece. I would if it were true, but it isn't. I got on with my life, had a great time writing, and so will you. Enjoy.

AD

PART I

Setting your objectives

1 Why publish?

Ideas are cheap. No one succeeds because they have good ideas. No single person ever became famous, rich or even promoted on the strength of an idea. It was because they did something with their idea that they reached their desired goal.

Have you ever heard people say that they're afraid to write about their research or give a conference paper because someone might steal their ideas? You might have even said it yourself. But, remember, an idea is just an idea. The theft of an idea is only a problem if the thief is going to do something with it. Maybe you have heard people say, on seeing some new invention, book title, TV show or such like, 'I thought of that years ago! If only I'd got round to doing something with it!'. The trouble is, they didn't. Someone else did, and that's what makes the difference.

There is a Japanese story of a Zen master who listened patiently to his student describe his current state of near-enlightenment: 'I've discovered, master, that all ideas are just false and artificial constructs!' The master nodded and replied: 'You can carry around that useless idea of yours if you want to.'

The only thing that counts is action. No one really cares about what you think. How would they know? They will only begin to care if you articulate it. If they want to 'steal' your thoughts, let them. Most of them will stay where you were before you decided to put your idea on paper. Most people's ideas stay as just that – ideas.

The world is filled with wannabees, wouldbees, shouldbees, and gosh-I-nearly-did-its. The worlds of academia and business are no different. Drawers upon drawers are filled with the beginnings of papers and books, halfhearted attempts to put words to paper, only interrupted by something *really* important, like the telephone ringing.

Let's not have any delusions about this. Getting published begins with the desire to do so, swiftly followed by action. Like anything else, it depends on your priorities. If your priority is to write, you will write. If it isn't, you probably won't. This book explores ways in which you can direct your energies and organize your priorities to best effect in getting your work published, but it can't manage your priorities for you.

There are many reasons to publish and just as many not to.

Why publish?

Clarity

'It helps me clarify my thinking,' say many authors. One is Bill Richardson, at Sheffield Hallam University, England, whose paper, 'Why we will probably not save mankind: a "natural" configuration of crisis-proneness', won the annual Best Paper Award in the *Disaster Prevention and Management* journal (Richardson, 1993). While Richardson's paper, which describes how human nature is basically crisis-prone and self-destructive, is somewhat pessimistic about the world in general, he is nothing but upbeat when he turns to the benefits of publishing.

Richardson, like many of the authors we'll meet in this book, is of the 'feel the fear but do it anyway' school. He claims that he will 'chain myself to the word processor' rather than let that empty screen get the better of him. If he doesn't, he explains, he just won't get around to it. There are always competing priorities but, at some point, writing has to become number one.

The process of writing is as important to him as the finished product. 'That's the most important reason to do it,' he says; it is even more important than the credibility it may give, or the benefits to an institution. By forcing yourself to sit down and put your ideas and evidence on paper, you find yourself refining them. Even better, you more easily see any flaws in your argument or methodology when they are staring you in the face. And who better to see them first than you?

Writing and revising are an education in themselves. We have to think through our ideas more carefully and structure them more logically as we write. Seeing our ideas or research findings in black and white allows us to confront the obvious and, at times, the obscure. Suddenly, a throwaway line leaps out at us and we think 'Yes! That's the whole point right there! I should put that point at the beginning, not lose it here in the middle'. Or, sometimes, we reread a paragraph or a phrase which makes us feel a little uneasy. It looks so emphatic on the page, but are we really sure we can be so positive about it? Maybe we ought to check our facts again – or at least express the thought in slightly different terms.

Choosing the right words and the right order all takes time, but most of that time is spent in preparation before we sit down to write. Planning may take weeks but, as we explain later in the book, the writing itself need never take more than a few days. A story about Abraham Lincoln illustrates this very point. He agreed to give a speech and was asked how much time he needed to prepare. He suggested that he would need a few days for a 20-minute speech, a week for a ten-minute speech, but if they wanted the speech to last two hours then he was ready immediately!

Revisiting

Ten years ago I created distance learning materials for a course run by a leading Australian logistics academic, John Gattorna, then a professor at Macquarie University, Sydney. My job was to organize all his material, draft out sessions for him to read and edit, and interview him regularly to get further ideas and direction. I remember once sitting with him in his office as he read through one of my drafts in which I had faithfully listed the five constituents of the logistics activity. He shook his head and muttered, 'Are there really only five, still? I need to work on this. There's another one, maybe another two', and off he went, revising standard logistics theory until he felt he had it right. And then there were seven.

It was the process of rereading his own work, with the goal of double-checking it, that caused the field to expand. Writing was merely the event. Writing helps us revisit our ideas and theories and look at them again in a fresh, more impartial way. There's nothing like seeing your idea in black and white to make you take it seriously. Did I really say that? Am I sure about this?

Usually, to get it right, you have to get it wrong first. To achieve a finished draft, you have to go through a first and second draft. Manufacturers call it concurrent engineering; working it out as you go, restructuring, revising, adding, subtracting – in other words, learning.

There is a great temptation to put off writing until you think you have the perfect paper to write. A prolific and award-winning author, Christian Grönroos of the Swedish School of Economics, remembers the advice given to him by his own supervisor: 'There are only two types of articles; those that are perfect and never get published, and those that are good enough and do.'

During the process of writing a paper, whether empirically based or conceptual, you will have the opportunity to re-examine your method, implications, discussion, findings and all the other components of an academic paper. You may often choose to alter sections then, or you may most likely decide it is good enough for now, send it away for publication, and continue to refine your approach for the next paper. In either case, you have had the opportunity to review your work and either make improvements or note those points which you need to work on next time.

Feedback

In all likelihood someone will comment on your work either when you show your draft to colleagues or after the paper is published. Of course, that's a very good reason why some people are reluctant to publish, but we'll examine that later. Let's look at the benefits first.

If your field of interest is growing – and let's hope it is – it grows by people adding their evidence and theories as they examine it. Your contribution causes other people to look at the field in a different way and, when they tell you about it, they are adding their ideas or evidence to yours. Another person's perspective can enrich yours. And, if another perspective causes you to reconsider, or even discard, your theory or idea, that's no problem. It is merely another road you've seen and chosen not to take and you can be thankful that someone pointed it out before you lost your way.

Feedback can lead to collaboration from unexpected sources. Those of us who surf the turbulent waves of the Internet know that already. Of course, our mailbox sometimes becomes cluttered with irrelevant messages, but there's often a gem lurking amongst the debris. Once published, you begin to meet people who know you through your writing. 'I saw your paper in such-and-such journal' a total stranger may say at a conference and will probably offer a constructive comment or another source of information you hadn't considered.

Feedback from others gives the lie to the old expression that you can't get something for nothing. Consider the refereeing process. Referees are anonymous authorities, appointed by editors, who will recommend that your piece of work will be accepted as is, rejected or should be revised and resubmitted. Most experienced authors welcome the 'revise' instruction, almost as much as a straight acceptance. 'Revise' feedback usually includes precise comments about which parts of the paper should be revised, and often how. We'll discuss the whole nature of refereeing later but, for now, it's enough to point out that the referee is most likely to be a respected leader in your particular field, who is freely giving an opinion on how you can improve your work. And it costs nothing.

Self-worth

There are many theories about human motivation. Behavioural psychologist Abraham Maslow said it was all about needs satisfaction which he neatly described as a hierarchy:

1   Survival – food, warmth
2   Safety – security, protection
3   Belongingness – social acceptance
4   Esteem – social recognition
5   Self-actualization – creativity, spirituality.

According to this theory, you can't paint while you're worrying about where your next meal is coming from. A little simplistic when you think about it, but it can suit as a reason to publish and not publish, and it's a reason many people give to explain their inability to make a start. 'I've a lot of things on my mind right now, but in a month or two I'll be less pressured,' they might say. We have all said that, only to find that the months roll on and we're as pressured as ever, taking care of the basics and thinking we can't devote time to the pressure to publish.

By actually publishing your work you will see tangible evidence that you're clever. There's no harm in that. Indeed, it can boost your self-confidence to the point where you'll probably rush to your word processor eager to start the next paper. Nothing breeds success like success, and seeing your name in print gives a satisfying frisson of excitement. And don't tell me you don't send a copy to your mum!

When, later on, we explore how to target journals, a number of techniques will be discussed. For now, it's wise to remember that, not surprisingly, the most sought-after journals have the highest rejection rates. It therefore makes good sense not to aim too high at first. There are more journals than you may know about these will be easier to get into, with editors and reviewers who have more time to discuss your work with you. With the constantly growing numbers of journals, and the increasing popularity of electronic publishing, there are likely to be several respectable, accessible journals in any given field that the aspiring author can try. Although famous authors will often say that they lived for years with rejections, not many of us want to do that just to make the manufacturers of antidepressants rich. Be kind to your frail ego and don't start by aiming at the stars. It's possible, but it's crowded up there.

Net worth

Publishing itself rarely makes anyone rich, unless you're Jeffrey Archer or Jackie Collins, but there are tangible benefits that arise as a result.

Research funding has become increasingly tied to published results. Although you might worry that you won't be accepted by the journals with the highest impact factors, working through the other journals will help you refine your approach, improve your style and make it more likely that, sooner rather than later, you will become published where you want. Having your papers published makes you more sought after for other reasons too, depending on your field: conferences, workshops, speeches and consultancy are all ways to make money to pay for further research. Some publishers and other organizations give awards for best papers, either as cash prizes, scholarships, research funding or products.

Promotion

It's fair to say those who manage to be published in the best journals are good, and that good people achieve success in the world, or at least they do in academic institutions that use the publications list as a guide to promotion. Are such people really so smart? Yes, but not just because they're intellectually advanced, but because they're smart with their time management. They've recognized the importance of publishing and got on with it, which is another reason they deserve promotion.

And do they know something you don't know? Yes, to that as well. They know how to write good papers and how to target the right journals. They know how to prioritize. They know how to transfer ideas from their heads on to paper where others can see, and be impressed by, them. By the time you finish this book you'll know too, because they'll be telling you in the pages that follow. They're not worried you'll steal their ideas. They've made it. So can you.

Institutional

Your college or university needs you. More than ever before, institutions are being held accountable for their outputs. One of the measures being applied is the number of papers published in quality journals. Increasingly, institutions are including publishing obligations in contracts. They want to make sure that the people they hire will not just promise to publish, as everyone does, but will actually do it. Although there is opposition in some circles to this requirement, many well respected scholars and authors welcome it because they know that everyone has the time, if they manage it properly, and that elevating the stature of the institution benefits everyone.

Body of knowledge

Whatever your field, from marketing research to embryonics, you belong to a body of knowledge. The field only grows because people add to it – people like you, who have something to say. If they didn't, the field would atrophy, become stale and perhaps die altogether. That doesn't mean everything you say must be brilliant or paradigm-busting. Perhaps your contribution is to revisit the body of knowledge with a new perspective or perhaps it's only to synthesize what has remained unsynthesized. At the very least, perhaps all you will do is clarify the current position, or cause a minor stir that can provoke debate.

Either way, it's a matter of making the choice of whether to be in or out of it – whether to fish or cut bait, as my American colleagues say. Are you a passenger, or do you add your own energy to driving the machine? You are paid to teach in that body of knowledge, paid to research about it and paid to contribute to it. Writing up your findings or articulating your concepts is an obligation.

Concurrent publishing

It's worthwhile to explore here an issue that stimulates some controversy in academic circles. Is it sensible, or even ethical, to publish portions of your research before it is finally complete? The schools of thought are these:

1   No, it isn't. The requirement for a PhD is that it is original work on submission, and how can it be original if some of it has appeared in a journal already?
2   Yes, it is. That a small portion of early research work has appeared does not detract from the originality of the whole. The portion could be accepted as a working paper or a research note, and the benefits of feedback to the student's research far outweigh any other concern.
3   It still isn't. A small portion of the total research does not benefit anyone. It's like teasing them with half the story when the final line is: 'We're carrying on with the research now; watch this space'.
4   It still is. If more researchers communicated more at interim stages, the whole field would move faster. Readers may not know the ultimate conclusions, but the approach taken or the interpretation of the literature may enrich their own work.

Much research, mostly scientific, is extremely money-hungry and therefore highly competitive. People in those fields are often reluctant to share their early findings for fear that their colleagues working elsewhere on the same issue will see what they're doing and use it to accelerate their own research. The ethics of people not communicating, especially in medical research, is another debate entirely, but the objections to 'publish-as-you-go' are often fuelled by fear.

Those who are so affected, and few are, will have to decide what is best for themselves. My advice is to check with your supervisors, sponsors and research coordinators who will usually be the best judge of whether the potential threats of publications outweigh the opportunities. Just make sure you're not using it as an excuse not to publish. After all, there are many more excuses available, as we shall see in the next chapter.

Action points

Each chapter in this book will conclude with a task which will help you shape your ideas for publication. You can do it right now or, if you want to read on further, do it later. But do it soon, even if you revise and change it later on. Use a notebook, or make a file on your PC, to keep the notes you make. When taken together they will create a plan for you to work through every time you write an article for publication.

Write a list of five to ten benefits to you of becoming published. Benefits are things that mean something to you. They might be personal benefits, such as: 'I would like to see my name in a well respected journal', or they might be professional benefits such as 'Writing an article about my research will expose it to others and might bring me speaking engagements or consultancy work'. Consider the benefits to your organization, such as how getting an article published will increase your research ratings, or appease your head of department or publicize the good work you have been doing. You might choose career benefits: 'I need to be able to list some good publications on my CV before I make my next job application' or any other kind of relevant benefits.

These are your objectives, the end-products of becoming published, the reasons you will make the time to craft your ideas into some well chosen words. Review them now and again, and change or add to them.

2 Why not publish?

There are as many good reasons not to publish as there are to publish. When I run workshops on getting published, I always make sure people in the audience tell me all the reasons they know not to publish as well as the reasons they should. That's because it is more useful to discover why we don't do things we want to than it is to nag ourselves with all the reasons we should. One approach makes us feel guilty and apathetic while the other may help remove the obstacles and spur us into action.

Fear

Fear is the most common reason people give for not publishing. There may be many more excuses, but when they really clear their throats and decide to be honest, it's fear that they admit to.

So why are they afraid? Margaret Redfern became an award-winning author when her paper 'I wannabe: the framework for continuing professional development' was judged the best in the 1993 volume of the *Librarian Career Development* journal (Redfern, 1993). When I asked her why she thought more people didn't publish, she answered: 'It's the fear of judgement.' How did she know? Because she has experienced it. Even the most experienced authors, in any field, will admit to being afraid sometimes. What if people laugh? What if they say that all the work we feel so good about is actually completely off-base? What if someone has done it all before?

Everyone has fears about all sorts of things, and some of the fears we have are ancestral and useful. A rush of adrenaline if we're alone in a dark

11

house and hear someone moving around downstairs is useful, but it's not so good if we've never yet met a burglar, we've locked all our doors and yet we still lie awake night after night worrying.

A field in psychology called cognitive behaviour explores how people convert thought to emotion and back again. Therapists try to help people distinguish between irrational thoughts creating inappropriate emotions from rational thoughts which reflect a more balanced view of the issue. The objective is to test the thoughts that are creating the emotion, giving them a 'reality check'. What lies behind the fear people have about getting published? Can we subject these fears to a reality check?

There's a simple exercise you can apply to test your own fears. On a sheet of paper, note the precise thought you have when the fear of publishing sweeps over you. Is it that you are a bad writer? Is it that you think people will dismiss your work outright? Is it perhaps a fear that they will criticize it for being shallow? Or that maybe they will steal your ideas and claim them as their own? Now, how strongly do you believe these thoughts right now? One hundred per cent? Seventy? Write it down.

Recording your fears is a positive step in your own publishing development. It means you are no longer procrastinating meekly, but are actually taking steps to overcome the most significant inhibitors facing new authors – fear. Make sure you use the opportunity to commit them all to paper, however foolish they may seem. Some day, when you feel like sharing them, you may be surprised to see how many of them appear on other people's lists.

The next step is to examine each fear more carefully and subject it to analysis. Let's take a few of them and see how they might stand up to closer inspection.

'I can't write!'

How bad a writer can you be? You got through school and into university, didn't you? Have you ever managed to express yourself on a birthday card or in a love letter? Did the recipients understand the message? Of course they did. Did you fail every essay or paper sent in for marking, on the grounds that they were incomprehensible? Of course you didn't.

So what exactly is the problem? The word 'bad', at the very least, might be changed to 'mediocre' or 'inconsistent'. Is that what you must accept? No.

Perhaps writing doesn't come easily to you; perhaps you don't find the words miraculously flowing from your fingertips. That's okay. No one else does either, not even professional writers. There are only three attributes which separate good writers from mediocre writers:

- preparation
- practice
- patience.

All of those are skills you can develop, and this book will show you how. Now, if you can see that your writing can't be truly bad, but may need developing, and you can see that there are ways to develop it, what does that do to your fear?

Note again on your paper the key points that helped reduce your fear and make a note of how much you now believe your first statement, 'I can't write'. Twenty per cent? Ten per cent? Finally, note the action or actions you plan to take. We waste far too much time worrying about our fears.

'They'll dismiss my work outright!'

Will they? Why should they? Is it a poor piece of research? What do your colleagues say? How did your supervisor or client or sponsor like it? In Chapter 3 we will see how to determine the real implications of your research. Authors often fail to describe them because they have not seen them themselves. For now, examine as you did in the first question exactly why you are afraid. Once again, subject this fear to analysis. Are people in your field really confident that they know it all? Would they not read with interest another person's contribution? Didn't your supervisor say it was good, and hasn't he or she seen many more before you? Haven't your colleagues supported you? The answer to all these questions is likely to be 'yes', for even a reasonable piece of work. That it may not change the world is not the point right now. If it helps people to look at it a little differently, that's enough.

If your piece of research really is substandard, or if your new conceptual framework hasn't grown beyond the rough sketch stage, you may be better off not publishing right now. You must, however, test that assumption thoroughly with trusted colleagues, because you may be underestimating your own work. That's very different from publishing, say, a paper about a common error you made in your research, from which you are learning and which you are willing to share with others.

One of the benefits of electronic publishing is that you can receive prompt feedback from other people, most of whom you have never met. If you are still nervous about the quality of your research, consider submitting a short note to one of the electronic journals or conferences available on the Internet. It's likely that you will receive at least some e-mail about your piece. Internet fora are good places to test and share ideas. You may find another researcher on the other side of the world interested in your work.

Finally, remember that criticism is one of the arts of academic life. Everyone learns to use critical reasoning powers, and therefore it would be unusual for someone not to look on your work critically, as you look on the work of others. But, that does not mean they will reject it outright, although it does mean they might, even should, evaluate it critically. Would you expect any less of your peers or your students? We know from our own experience of evaluating research that we are not criticizing the person when we criticize the work. We can therefore rest assured that criticism of our own work will be fully in the spirit of academic enquiry. If we have done all the right preparation and have passed the final review stages, we do not need to fear that anyone will dismiss our work at a glance.

Review now how strongly you believe your original statement that people will reject your work outright. It probably isn't a reasonable fear, once you think about it. What's it worth – 10 per cent? What is your plan of action to further reassure yourself?

'People will steal my ideas'

As we saw in Chapter 1, this fear forms part of the 'publish as you go' debate. Fear of theft by unscrupulous ideas burglars can probably be left to disturb the sleep of a scientist who is about to discover the cure for AIDS and therefore stands to gain riches and international prestige in the process. For the rest of us, we can generally assume that other people are busy working out their own ideas and, however brilliant and original we think our ideas are, they think theirs are, too.

In worrying about people stealing ideas we are evading an important principle of academic work – isn't its purpose to disseminate knowledge? Writing in *The Independent* on 30 August 1995, Sir Douglas Hague (Associate Fellow, Templeton College, Oxford), put it succinctly:

> The whole point of academic research, of course, is that its findings should not be opaque and inaccessible, but available to those who could benefit from them – not least those outside universities. That is why I am constantly amazed, and increasingly frustrated, by the resistance of researchers to the insistence that disseminating research findings is at least as important task as was reaching them in the first place.

It seems that the real issue is the matter of attaching one's name to the research findings. With a clear strategy worked out, which we will explore in later chapters, you do not have to fear that people won't credit you for your work. After all, we know exactly who discovered the four laws of motion, who created the law of relativity, where the term 'pasteurized' comes from and the name of the man who first mass-produced cars.

'I don't know where to start!'

This fear relates to one of our oldest and most primitive – the fear of the dark. How can we push ourselves into an abyss, into a huge gaping black hole called 'publishing' when we don't know enough about it? How will we know that our papers will stand up to the scrutiny of the editor and his or her review board? How will we even know to which journal to send it? How will we start to write? How long will it take? Will we ever finish it?

Few people take pleasure in being lost. Publishing is a mysterious process, but it is one that anyone can understand, learn and master. This is the central thesis of this book, but it isn't your only source of help. Attending writers' workshops, meeting colleagues who have published, and talking to people who edit and review journals will help demystify the publishing business and help you write the kind of papers which will eventually be published.

For now, the answers to the following questions are brief:

- *How can I push myself into an abyss ...?* You don't. The first rule of a successful publishing strategy is to do your homework. Most papers fail because the writer has not considered the needs of the journal and its readers. The following chapters will show you how.
- *How will I know that my papers will stand up to the scrutiny of the editor and review board?* By following the straightforward guidance of reviewers, editors and other authors, either by contacting them directly, or learning from their ideas distilled in the pages of this book.
- *How will I start?* By thinking through a few main points discussed later, concentrating on purpose, implications and the right target journal.
- *How long will it take?* To do what? To write before undertaking the initial preparatory stage? A few months, maybe years, possibly forever. After spending some directed preparation time and then writing? A couple of days.
- *Will it ever be finished?* The paper, yes. The ongoing quest for perfection, no.

The need for perfection

Recall the advice of the doctoral supervisor quoted in the previous chapter: 'There are only two types of articles; those that are perfect and never get published, and those that are good enough and do.'

The need to be perfect inhibits many people who don't put their words to paper. There's always one more edit that will make it right, always one more piece of information, always one more question to answer. But, how can you create perfection if you don't create at all? All any of us can do, as my good old Dad used to say, is our best. 'Best' includes being aware of the sell-by date. The perfect article may indeed be perfect, two years after everyone else in the field has moved on. It might be so perfect that you can frame it page by page in your study. Indeed, why not think of other ornaments you can make with the pages of unfinished, nearly perfect articles? As we saw earlier, the competition in this market is fierce. As you are patiently perfecting your article, there will probably be two or three people licking the envelopes enclosing papers similar to yours. They'll be published in six months while you're still seeking another reference.

What's the worst that can happen?

What if, with all your best efforts behind you, your paper is returned to you, either asking for revisions or informing you politely that it is simply not acceptable at all?

Even the best authors have been rejected. If that's the worst that happens, is it really so bad? There's always the possibility that another journal might accept what the first has rejected, not because its standards are different but because the needs at the time are different. And even if every journal rejects it, what does this really tell you? At worst it means you need to do some more work on the topic. That's no problem. After all, that's your job – researching and contributing to the body of knowledge. Just as not all of your students will get an 'A', so not all of your papers will hit the mark.

More likely, if you've done your homework, you will be asked to revise your paper before it can be accepted for publication. We will discuss this in more detail in Chapter 13, but the most important point is never to forget that the comments from an editorial review are free, honest and of high quality. Welcome the opportunity to revise as a learning experience; it's a positive activity, not one to fear or be embarrassed about.

Priorities

'I'm too busy!' you say. Of course you are. And so are the authors who are being published right now in your field. If being published is important to you, you will find the time. But first, consider what you mean by time. Is it time spent nervously staring at the word processor going nowhere? Or time, maybe an hour each day, putting your thoughts on paper and organizing your approach?

The Performance Group in Oslo (Bjelland et al., 1994) studied similarities amongst those described as peak performers – writers, musicians, politicians, academics and industrialists. Amongst their several shared characteristics was their ability to concentrate intensely on whatever they were doing. They quote the Nokia Chief Executive Jorma Ollila saying: 'If someone focuses on what they are doing, they can do in 15 minutes what would otherwise take me four hours.'

Taking time to write necessarily means taking significant blocks of time, but it is more important to manage the quality of the time rather than the quantity. Successful, prolific authors are probably as busy as, or busier than, you are. They may only block out one hour every two days to work on their manuscript, but in that time they are able to concentrate on what they are doing. The question, therefore, is not 'How much time do I have?' but 'How can I use the time I have most effectively?'.

The better time management courses don't simply teach about what letters to open and how to delegate. They teach about knowing what your priorities are and how to get on with them. If the project matters to you, you will find the time.

Summary

These first two chapters have drawn together some of the most common reasons people give for why they should, or should not, publish. Each point has a flip side: the benefits of people knowing about your work does open up the possibility that they may not approve of it. This, as we have seen earlier, is the nature of learned debate and not something to take personally.

The central issue is 'going public': the word 'publish' derives from the Latin *publicare*, to make public. It is not without reward, and it is not without risk. Today, it is becoming less of an option and more of an expectation, whilst at the same time the competition is increasing and the standards are rising. Fortunately, the process is well understood and can be managed.

Each of us has different incentives in mind and experience different constraints. Before going much further, you might like to note your own reasons for publishing and all the reasons which have prevented you so far. It is then a matter of concentrating on the benefits and seeing how you can minimize the risks. After all, people who have no fear are not brave, they are fearless. Bravery is having the fear but doing it anyway.

Action points

Note any excuses you used for not turning your ideas into publishable articles. List no more than six and, for each one, note your feelings then think of a counterargument that you really believe, a conclusion about the barriers and the counterargument, and the action you can take to break through any fears you might have. For example:

- I can talk about my ideas, but I become stuck when I try to write them down (*thought*).
- That makes me feel worried about exposing something I've written to an audience (*feeling*).
- But the restructuring paper I wrote last year at work was very well received, and everything I argued for was accepted (*counterargument*).
- I can express my ideas if I care about something, and think carefully about my audience (*conclusion*).
- I need to start with something I'm really interested in, that will be of benefit to me, and consider carefully who will be reading it (*action*).

Any time you reach a block, or feel less than confident, go back and look at your 'fears' list. Add to the counterarguments and the conclusions. If another block arises, add it to your list and analyse your way through it using the same framework.

3   A sense of purpose

There's an old adage that says if we don't know where we are going, any road will do. But, if we have our destination firmly in mind, we can search out and use maps to help us navigate.

Ask professional writers to sit down and write a few thousand words and they will start asking questions. A few thousand words about what? A few thousand words for whom? A few thousand words to achieve which objective? Yet, many novice writers complain that they cannot sit down to write a few thousand words because they are suffering from 'writer's block'. The expression is a strange one that means little to professional writers. Were they to wait for some mystical muse to sprinkle a little fairy dust on their PC they would still be waiting, but they're not. They are the ones with their pieces finished and published while everyone else is waiting for their mysterious writer's block to melt away.

Unfortunately, writing seems mysterious to those who don't do it regularly. It seems that people who don't write regularly can conclude that they are not writers. How often have you heard someone say, or said yourself, 'I'm not a writer', as if a writer is a completely separate breed. For those who do write, especially for those who earn their living at it, it's a job like any other. Sometimes their writing would not escape the critical scrutiny of the average English Literature undergraduate. Take a closer look at how people like Jeffrey Archer, Jackie Collins or Barbara Cartland write. The quality of the prose can be mediocre, even poor at times, but the story itself, the pace and the well developed characterizations captivate millions of readers. These are writers who know what they are going to say, and work hard at it, every day. As

Thomas Edison once said, genius is one-per cent inspiration and ninety-nine per cent perspiration.

Writers don't have blocks. They may have lost the thread of what they are trying to say, they may realize that they need more information about a certain point which they will fill in later, but they are not blocked by an extraordinary force beyond their control. People who have writer's block are really being blocked by a lack of understanding about what needs to be said. They have lost their focus.

Back to basics

It is surprising, considering that we have all at some stage gone through primary school, that so much can be forgotten about our first lessons in communication. It seems that once we enter university we somehow think we can no longer follow the simple rules we learned at school. Indeed, for some people, the very idea that communication should follow simple rules seems to contradict the ethos of higher education. Suddenly, our language becomes more convoluted and dreary, we find ourselves reaching for the thesaurus to find a longer word which will replace the shorter, more familiar word and, worst of all, our writing seems to turn into a game we're playing with the reader: if we really waffle on for five thousand words using the most syllables per sentence we can find, and if we ramble our way through the paper with no obvious sense of direction, will we trick our reader into thinking that we are more clever than he or she?

No. Our readers, if we should be so lucky to escape the remonstrations of editors and reviewers first, will simply become frustrated and bored. They will never discover the essential quality of the research or the benefits it may confer on them. They will give up or, if they are forced to read it through a tutor's direction or the demands of their own research, they won't like it much.

This chapter and the next two deal with the two criteria of quality that span all disciplines and all forms of papers. These chapters represent the most compelling implication of the research carried out by the author and colleagues into academic publishing (Day and Peters, 1995). What we discovered was simple, but sometimes not easy to apply. All other qualities being met, the two most important concerns of reviewers are:

- What is this paper about?
- Why does it matter?

Editors will return papers for revision or reject them simply because the author or authors did not explain why they were writing the paper and what it all means. Sometimes, that's because they have not considered for themselves the purpose of the paper, other than perhaps to meet a demand to publish. They have not moved beyond the level of analysis we covered in Chapters 1 and 2. They have determined that publishing is important and they have motivated themselves sufficiently to write something, but they have not considered the purpose of the paper or its implications from the readers' perspectives. Ultimately, they have failed to communicate.

As the pressure to publish increases and the flow of papers on to an editor's desk increases, the editor may spend less time reading any single paper. In these circumstances, all the best editorial intentions in the world cannot create more time to decide whether a paper is worth reading. Faced with several alternatives to achieve the same goal – that is, several papers on the same subject from the same sort of people – the editor will naturally prefer the ones that are most accessible. If it is not immediately apparent what the paper is about, who can blame the weary editor who puts it aside, only to find that the next paper down in the pile fits the journal's needs on that particular topic precisely? The one that was too vague to be appreciated will be sent back with a kindly note advising the author that the journal has met its requirements on the subject. At best, the editor may send the paper to a reviewer for an initial appraisal only to receive the same conclusion, or a request to revise the paper radically. Either way, everyone has wasted time.

At authors' workshops, and in meetings with researchers, I ask everyone to complete a simple test to judge the quality of an article. Papers on a wide variety of subjects, some of which will be completely unfamiliar to the audience, are circulated with the understanding that participants will only have five minutes to look through them. Some will be a few pages long; others will be 15 or 20. The participants are asked to scan the article quickly and note down the purpose, its key points and its implications. It quickly becomes obvious that some authors are able to state their purpose clearly in the first few paragraphs, provide obvious signposts to guide the reader to the main points, and include clear statements of why the article will be important to researchers or practitioners. Others, sometimes from less reputable journals with few submissions from which to choose, fail to do so. I know which I find easiest to read and which, as an editor, I would be more likely to recommend for publication.

The point of the exercise is not to claim deep and meaningful understanding of the subject, which may require several rereadings and careful thought, but to be able to assess whether the paper is worth reading at all. This is what editors, reviewers and readers actually do. In most fields, with the exception of a few highly specialized areas, there is a plethora rather than a paucity of information. If the busy reader cannot immediately grasp the purpose and the main points of a paper, he or she will automatically choose an alternative – that is, of course, assuming that the paper has survived the editors' and reviewers' first reading. The following examples are direct quotations from reviewers' reports, several of hundreds the author has collected during research for this book:

- 'Lacks a sense of purpose'
- 'Author does not explain why he is writing this paper'

- 'Not clear where paper is going or why'

Clearly, we want to avoid receiving those kinds of comments. Let's see how.

How far do you go?

Many authors stumble over the purpose of the paper because they have not made up their own minds about how far they can go in pursuing their research question. This is often a flaw in their original research design. No one can answer all the related questions about an issue and stay focused, but they can acknowledge that those questions exist while they concentrate on a particular aspect. Such an approach dictates what is known as the scope of the study, just as the scope of an instrument, such as a telescope, allows us to see only to a certain distance.

If, for example, you were to study how to evaluate the effectiveness of training programmes in, say, the health service, you would have to confine yourself to the health service itself. You could not, however, approach that topic without first understanding the nature of training itself and how it is evaluated. In the same way, you would confuse your reader if you suddenly launched into health service training issues without first putting him or her in the picture.

Authors frequently fear that what they are saying about one field – such as the effectiveness of training in the health service – will be criticized by others who might say that the same conclusions would not apply in, say, the military field. That fear can lead to a vagueness of purpose in the paper because the author tries to mask his or her lack of knowledge about wider application issues rather than meet it head on and state it. This can be avoided by stating clearly that the scope of the research has been limited to the health service and suggesting that future studies on, say, training in the public sector as a whole, might build on and further the author's research.

Once the author clearly explains the scope, he or she can continue by acknowledging the related areas which have not been discussed but may be relevant. These can often be usefully cited by such phrases as: 'While it is beyond the scope of this paper to adequately cover the work on training evaluation in the private sector, readers are referred to the work of ...'

Having defined the scope of the project, the researcher either immediately or subsequently then faces constraints that affect the course of the study. These are commonly known as limitations. Time and money will limit the study, as will other constraints such as data availability. Some of these may not be evident at the beginning of the research but the author must state if they later arose and affected the validity of the findings. The scope and limitations of the original research will be the same as those expressed in the paper. The paper itself, being perhaps a 5000-word distillation of a dissertation several times longer, has limitations of its own, which again need explanation. Before beginning to refine the purpose statement of the paper, make sure you have noted the scope and limitations that will guide the paper. The following questions may help.

1   Scope:

- How far did I decide to look?
- What influenced that decision?
- What related issues did I not examine and why?
- Will I go on to examine those?
- Where can I guide the reader who wants to examine the related issues?
- To what extent can I generalize my conclusions?

2   Limitations:

- What constraints did I impose and why?
- Which were imposed on the work and why?
- Which were unexpected?
- How do they affect the validity of the study?
- How can future researchers, or I, vary them?

Authors usually find that once they have answered questions such as those above they feel more confident about defining the purpose of the paper. Restrictions and limitations influence us, but do not necessarily reduce the contribution we make. The critical point is to be clear about what those restrictions are, and tell the reader.

Twenty words or less

Someone once said that if you can't describe your view of the world, your religion or your philosophy in less than a minute, it's probably not worth saying. A weakness of many learned articles is that the writer either had no clear idea of the paper's purpose, or did, but did not know how to express it. Before going any further into planning your paper, make sure you know the answer to the questions:

- What do you want to say?
- Why should anyone care?

Why do you want to write the paper? We've already discussed some of the reasons, from the personal to the institutional perspective, in Chapter 2, but here we need to concentrate on the research or concept itself. The only purpose that is of interest to your reader is that your paper has something to say. That 'something' is likely to include at least one or more from the following list.

- It adds conceptually to the current body of knowledge through new thinking.
- It adds empirically to the current body of knowledge through new evidence.
- It exposes a weakness in the current body of knowledge.
- It demonstrates a new way of applying the body of knowledge.

Implicit in all the above are the usual processes and standards you must apply. The research methodology must be robust, your literature review must be thorough and appropriate, your writing must be clear, and so on. But these alone are not enough. If your paper lacks purpose and implication, it will be just another routine review of either concept or evidence.

The first step is to write in 20 words or less your purpose in writing this paper. They will not be necessarily the exact words used in the paper itself – although many papers would be improved by opening in just this way – but will help you clarify your own approach. You will revisit this purpose each time you consider a separate audience, to ensure that you modify the salient points for the benefit of your target group. (We will discuss later how understanding the audience will help you position your papers to make them relevant to different groups of readers.) Any piece of research, however, will have begun with a purpose of some sort, either to prove, disprove or extend. The following examples show how you might write a simple statement describing the purpose of your paper.

- 'I show how misinterpreting Smith's early work leads to wrong conclusions and weak hypotheses.'
- 'I describe our evidence that molecular behaviour is not erratic in circumstances that others term chaotic.'
- 'I provide my conceptual model linking customer service to internal team building.'
- 'I show how Porter's model transforms health care administration in Iowa.'

If the above examples sound a little too bold, read how other authors have expressed their purpose in their finished paper:

> In this paper, we report consequences of odor learning in a situation where this parasitoid has a choice between the learned odor and an alternative one. We also consider the influence of odor concentration, which is an important factor in odor learning by the honeybee. (Kaiser and De Jong, 1995)

Is there any doubt that we can expect to find important conclusions about how honeybees learn to differentiate smells? Our next example is equally clear about its purpose, but also clear about its conclusiveness:

> This paper, therefore, has two linked purposes: to review recent scholarship on women's role in welfare and, through an analysis of the juvenile court movement,

one of the major social welfare reforms of the Progressive Era, to identify issues of controversy and debate among historians of women and welfare. (Clapp, 1994)

The above statement leaves no room for ambiguity. We know we can expect to understand what other contemporary researchers have said about women's role in welfare, and that the author will share, through a specific analysis, an understanding about certain outstanding questions. It does not tell us that the writers have formed conclusions of their own, but if we are studying women's issues, welfare issues or both, we can assume that the article will be providing a helpful context of the state of research. The next example is similarly clear about the purpose, while also being careful to point out its scope:

The purpose of this report is to discuss the nature and consequences of the dominating marketing paradigm of today, marketing mix management of the managerial school (cf.25) and how evolving trends in business and modern research into, for example, industrial marketing, services marketing and customer relationship economics demand a relationship-oriented approach to marketing ... Finally, the possibility of building a general theory of marketing based on the relationship approach is examined. (Grönroos, 1994)

Once again, we know the author's direction. Interestingly, the above two examples show us that the authors do not intend to give us a final answer to the question being explored. They are opening up a line of enquiry and inviting us to explore it. Note the caveat in the last example: 'the possibility of building a general theory of marketing ...'. This indicates the author's decision about the scope of the paper, which happened to win the journal's annual Best Paper Award.

Fear of focus

Thus far we have seen how authors state their purpose and have examined a few helpful techniques. Besides being unaware of these techniques, however, authors sometimes have further reasons to resist clearly stating their intent. If we clearly state our purpose, we are leaving the reader in no doubt as to what we are going to say. That means we're going to have to say it! Worse, that means we can be criticized for not following through with the purpose. This criticism appears frequently on referees' reports: 'Authors claim they are going to add new evidence to the body of knowledge ... it's a pity they failed to do so.'

Ouch! That hurts. But a good editor will not reject your paper because your ideas are unconventional, or because a reviewer happens to hold an opinion other than the one you are expressing. Certainly, if you are proposing an idea that runs counter to the usual viewpoint, you had best make sure your argument is sound. But your papers are only liable to incur the kind of comment above if you do not deliver the promise you made – and you can't escape that promise.

Summary

A sense of purpose is crucial and fundamental. Editors reject papers that are vague and directionless. If what you have to say means you will be held to account for it, feel the fear and do it anyway. Some people will agree, some won't. Isn't that the nature of philosophic enquiry? If we always simply supported the existing way of thinking, our field would wither and die.

As a first step, ask yourself the following questions:

- Does my sense of purpose frighten me?
- What am I afraid of?
- Who am I afraid of?
- What's the worst that can happen if I publish it?
- What's the worst that can happen if I don't?

Part of the fear of focus is one we looked at in the last chapter – the fear of being imperfect. One way of overcoming the fear of imperfection is to be clear about your limitations and scope.

Finally, test out your purpose on other people. Make sure that anyone, including those not involved in your area of research, understands it. Make sure it's concise and to the point. Most importantly, make sure you can achieve it within the paper. It will act as your guide while you sketch out your outline and eventually choose the words to develop it.

Action points

Write down, in two or three sentences, the purpose of your planned paper. Start with the phrase 'The purpose of this paper is to ...'. Consider verbs such as 'show', 'demonstrate', 'present', 'synthesize', 'explore', 'review', 'discuss' and 'identify'. Make sure you are explicit about what you are trying to do. Then note how you are going to deliver the purpose: '... by illustrating with case examples ...'; '... by describing the results of an experiment conducted ...'; '... by reviewing the current literature on ...'

Congratulations! You have just written one of your opening paragraphs! Remember, however, to revisit your purpose statement as you develop your paper to make sure it still promises what you are delivering.

4   So what?

Now that you have a starting point – a purpose – you should consider what is its significance for others. This, once more, is a reflective process. When you have been immersed deeply in a piece of research it is easy to lose sight of its value for others who are not as familiar with the area. Even people working on the same issue will not have been privy to your approach and findings, until the article appears. The implications of what you have done may be obvious to you, but will it be obvious to anyone else?

Enter your readers' minds

Many researchers, even experienced authors, find it difficult to step back and look at their work from the reader's perspective. The reasons for this are varied but may often be the same concerns that confronted us when considering publishing at all: fear of judgement and the need for perfection.

Stating the implications of research is the moment when we crystallize the value of our work. This can be a disconcerting experience, for we are boldly setting out in black and white what we believe that other people should think about the work we have done. Wouldn't it be easier to let them draw their own conclusions? Easier, perhaps, but only in the short term. A paper lacking clear implications will usually be rejected or sent back for revision. Analysis of referees' reports and discussions with editors makes it clear that the implications factor is the criterion that transcends all other necessary, but insufficient, conditions that may have been met. We may show a reasonable literature review, proper research design, excellent execution, readability and so on, all of which are important, but are considered as only the entry point for a good academic paper. We need to move further. This is how one reviewer expressed it: 'Presented some facts and shown some differences, but has not shown that these findings are important.'

That is the type of article that might be expected from an undergraduate approaching a subject for the first time and needing to summarize what the relevant thinkers have written so far. There may even be a section describing something the author has observed but which he or she has so far not thought to interpret and analyse. It leads the reviewer to read the paper, shrug his or her shoulders and say, 'So what?'

Another reviewer commented:

> I would regard this as the application of existing theory to a stated problem – a consultancy type assignment. The paper is quite theoretical. It reads OK with little amendment. However, it is of limited application and I doubt whether you would wish to publish it.

Although we may fear that readers will disagree with our statement about our work's value, probably the biggest obstacle is, once more, our need to be perfect. We must appreciate the reader as someone whose interest in our work may only be peripheral, or who may even be a student approaching the subject for the first time. We may know that our research in the field is continuing, and that more answers will arise in the future, but where does that leave the reader? While we see our work as a continuum, the paper is an event that arises along that continuum and must be seen as a whole in its own right.

It may help to consider that point more fully, thereby easing our concern that the work may be as yet unfinished. A publishable paper must encapsulate the essence of what we have done thus far and draw out conclusions even as we stand on a moving line. Try to view it as a milestone, if not the end point. Explaining that to your readers will reassure both you and them that you have not yet reached the end of the line, but that significant implications are arising en route. The following example does just that:

> The objectives of this article are to suggest a basis by which the potential value of combinatorial strategies can be assessed, and to identify milestones that will help provide an interim evaluation. (Ecker and Crooke, 1995)

We could deal with this chapter in a similar fashion ... The purpose of this chapter is to explain why implications are important and suggest exercises that may help you to come closer to explaining the implications in your own work.

Implications are not reiterations

The objective here is not merely to summarize your work, which anyone can do, but to identify and articulate the worth of your work to others. This is making good the promise you made at the beginning of the article when you stated your purpose. Concluding the paper with a summary of findings is not the same as pointing out the impact of your work and how it will affect others. If you have contributed to the body of knowledge through new conceptual thinking, what will it matter? How have you contributed? Why should anyone care? How will they be able to use what you have discovered? If you have applied current thinking to a new area, what can anyone do about it? How will your work change anything in thought or practice? What, specifically, do further researchers or practitioners need to do next?

The implications of your work may be for research or practice, but they must be described. It is not your reader's job to try to decode what your significant message may be. You should say, clearly and in full, what you believe the implications of your analysis are to others. As we well know, the problem today in most fields is not a lack of information but a vast, often vague, morass of information through which we must painstakingly sieve. The better journals, and therefore the better authors, are those which cut through the sieving process for the readers and bring them straight to the point. As a reader we may choose to agree, to disagree, to adapt an author's ideas, to ignore them, or to follow them. That is up to us. Those responsible for judging those articles and bringing them from author to reader understandably become a little impatient with anything less than a straight answer to the obvious question: 'So what?'

The following example ably answers that all-important question:

> This study has shown that eight artefact-free 8-s epochs of data are sufficient to give internal consistency reliability coefficients around .9 for resting EEG power spectra of schizophrenics and normal subjects. (Lund *et al.*, 1995)

The reader is left in no doubt about the main findings and their implications, but also benefits further, as the authors go on to say, 'Because not all studies use 8-s epochs or site Cz, future research could assess how the duration of individual epochs or scalp site affects reliability'. Later, they indicate other avenues which might be taken by further research.

Implications of research

A statement of implications gives us a way to generalize our findings. Research that only applies to you personally in your own precise situation can be of no value to anyone else. One criterion facing postgraduate students is that they must contribute to the body of knowledge. Many wise supervisors explain that research must grow from the specific to the general so that other people can learn from it, apply it and take it forward. What are the steps that we need to take?

It may be useful at this point to review briefly what we mean by the research process. Any piece of research is built around a design, which begins with identifying a problem and then the issue that guides our understanding. The research problem is the specific question being examined by the researcher, such as 'can the culture of the public service adapt to performance reward techniques?'. The problem might arise from background to the research, such as previous researchers' flaws or superficialities, or it might arise from a specific question being imposed by a research client who is funding institutional research.

The implication for the reader will relate to the findings that answer the question as applied to the public service. It will include direction for those interested in implementing a performance reward system and may include direction for people carrying on further research in the area.

As most researchers know, problem definition is one of the most difficult stages of any research project. Some people carry on with inadequate problem identification and then face the difficulty of trying to redefine midway through the project or even afterwards. If they still have not defined it properly by the time they write their paper they are unlikely to please a reviewer who is left scratching his or her head and wondering what the fuss is about. One author who had not met these criteria caused a reviewer to comment:

> Introductory section is poorly structured, lacking clear problem definition. Conclusions could tie in more fully to some of the issues raised in the introduction.

The research problem is, however, not the whole story. No researcher can investigate a problem without understanding the context. The example below, therefore, reflects the direct question of the researcher about performance reward techniques in the public service, but could not be understood properly without the wider context of what we mean by 'performance reward' or what we mean by culture. These are the issues that enclose the problem. The implication will therefore relate to the issue itself and may give direction to other researchers in light of the new findings from the specific research.

Figure 4.1 illustrates this point diagrammatically and demonstrates that the author must attend to the implications of both the problem and the issue, where relevant. This is particularly important if the author mentions in the introduction why and how the research is important for others. If it is a problem that needs resolution, relating to a wider issue in the general body of knowledge, so what? Have you discovered anything that should be applied or understood by others? What are the implications of this particular research problem resolution, and what are the implications for the body of knowledge on the redefined issue?

Having properly identified the problem and issue, the research design then includes a method by which the research will gather relevant data.

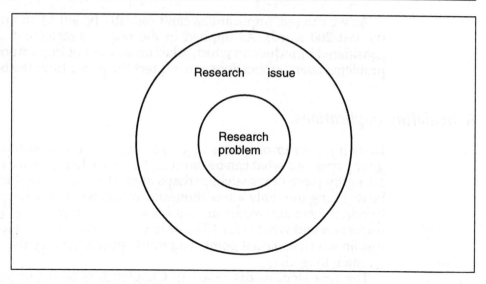

Figure 4.1: Issue and problem

What are the implications of that methodology? Are there implications simply for the particular researcher, or are they for others in the field? What, for example, are the implications of face-to-face interviews as opposed to questionnaires? What are the implications of a double-blind controlled trial? Why did we choose a certain data gathering technique rather than any other, and what limitations may arise as a result?

Once we have the data, we need to make sense of what we have found by turning data into intelligence. This is where we apply the data to the original question and analyse it. But, once again, we need to explain the implications of any analytical method we have chosen, for the process by which we interpret the data will determine how we make sense of it. Readers may disagree with our interpretation, but will be at a loss to know how we arrived at our own conclusions unless we tell them.

Finally, our analysis should lead us to a resolution of the problem in a way that makes sense for our readers. It is at this stage we will draw out the implications of our analysis to resolve the problem and to add further to the existing body of knowledge on the issue.

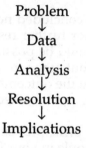

As we can see, implications can't casually be left as an afterthought in the last 200 words. As implied in the referee's statement above, an ill-considered introduction which takes no account of implications will cause problems later. Implications must direct the paper from the beginning.

Articulating implications

Knowing your implications helps you decide what should be included in your paper and what can be omitted. Particularly if you are writing about a lengthy piece of research, perhaps at masters or doctoral level, you will be distilling into only a few thousand words what may have taken you a hundred thousand words in your dissertation. How do you know what is important and what is not? The only way to answer that question is to be certain which essential points you must cover to convey the value of your research to readers.

The first step, as discussed in Chapter 3, is to define your purpose. Naturally following from that is to articulate the implications in the research – this is what I decided to do and this is how it matters.

- Step 1: Purpose. What is it and why does it matter?
- Step 2: Findings: What, for whom and how do they matter?

In Chapter 3 (page 24), an example illustrating clear purpose taken from the *Journal of American Studies* described the role of women in welfare and the juvenile court movement. It promised to review the recent relevant body of knowledge and to highlight areas of debate. Their conclusion was that new work suggests that a less 'male-centric' view of welfare is necessary, that men and women had different views about welfare; that women often led the initiatives; and that recent studies showed differences amongst middle class reformers. So what? Until this point we only have a summary of what their paper has already said. What is anyone to do next?

> Historians of women and welfare need therefore to look beyond the difference in visions of welfare between male and female reformers, to examine the nuances in maternalism itself. (Clapp, 1994)

The author has concluded not simply with a summary but with a direct guidance note for further research to be picked up by other researchers. None of that would be possible without first putting oneself in the reader's mind, without going through the questions that might occur to someone interested in the outcomes of the research.

Key questions can be asked here:

- What wider principles emerged from your research?
- How can people in your field use it?

- Can people in other fields use it?
- How can other researchers take your work forward?
- How can your research be applied in practice?

The answers to some of these questions may be 'don't know' or 'not applicable'. Which ones do apply, and what are your answers?

Finding more

Having tackled the two most important guides to implications – purpose and findings – try to look at the various components of your paper and articulate their implications. Each decision you have made needs to be explained. Implications in the literature are so important that Chapter 5 of this book is devoted entirely to writing a literature review with evaluative and analytical techniques which can help your reader. There are, however, many other sections of a paper that also have implications:

- What were the implications of your scope and limitations, discussed in the last chapter?
- What were the implications of choosing particular methods of data gathering and analysis?
- Did certain techniques cast some doubts or further veracity on your findings?

Two years ago, at a conference, I listened to an academic presenting research he had carried out on the potential impact of team management training in a professional practice. Apparently, after an exhaustive series of interviews with six partners in one practice he arrived at the conclusion that some professionals thought it was a good idea, some thought it wasn't, and there did not seem to be anything which indicated that their likes or dislikes related to their age, position, personal values or any other recognisable factor. So what? Yet what could have been a fairly dull and uneventful presentation turned into a lively debate as fellow academics began to question the speaker on the implications of the research design itself. Were six people sufficient? How were they chosen? How were they interviewed?

Prepare yourself a list of answers to the questions that might arise about the effect of your approach. Try to work out the implications not only of your significant findings but also the impact that your approach has had on the project itself and your conclusions.

Implication checklist

- **Purpose**. What is it and why does it matter?
- **Findings**. Why, for whom and how do they matter?

- **Literature**. What did it say and how does it matter to your research?
- **Methodology**. How did it affect the findings?
- **Analysis**. How did the techniques affect your findings?
- **Options**. What are the implications of potential answers to the problem?
- **Conclusion**. How far are you prepared to go and why?

As an exercise, take a few moments to note down, in 20 words or less, answers to the above questions. If you find this difficult, you will need to think longer and harder before approaching your paper. Once you have condensed your implications into 20 words or less you will be better able to review your work and decide what is important.

There's a saying in quality management circles that 'quality must be designed in from the beginning'. It's not an afterthought, but a starting point. We can say the same about implications. Knowing them can guide us through the paper and help us to reach a strong finish. At least we may be able to avoid the sting of another reviewer who wrote:

> The 'surprising result' would not have been particularly surprising if the authors had thought at the beginning of the study what they had expected to find.

Implementing implications

Whether research has implications for further research, immediate practice or both, consider carefully how the reader can use this knowledge in practice. Although your initial reaction might be that such direction lies outside the scope of the paper, who is in a better position than the original author to suggest how the reader might proceed further?

If we think through the point made earlier in this chapter, that the author is often someone who is continuing research, what specific steps are being laid out for other researchers or practitioners? Consider, for example, the reader as a PhD student reading the article and interested in taking some of the points further. By telling the reader how to do something useful with the findings, the author is making a chain for someone else to follow. What are the links in that chain?

Say, for example, that you have just concluded research on the success rate of implementing Total Quality Management (TQM) programmes in large organizations. Perhaps you studied five large companies, two of which succeeded and three of which failed. The single notable variable was the commitment, or otherwise, of top management. You therefore conclude that involving top management is key to the success of a TQM programme. That's the implication so far, but what is the reader to do about it?

At this stage you might make two suggestions, such as involving top management in the initial planning stages of the programme and debriefing them regularly on the programme's progress. Those are two actions that your reader might take, and therefore turns the paper from an interesting report to a practicable solution to a problem many people find with TQM.

When considering the useful outcomes of your research, run through the who, what, where, when and how questions that might provoke some answers or at least strong hints to give your readers:

- Who is able to apply your findings?
- What might they do?
- When and where might it be done?
- How might they approach it?

Too often, we leave the follow-through to our reader's imagination. Given our intense involvement in the question at hand, we ought to be able to offer more than an offhand 'go away and think about it' statement.

All of the above means that authors must think through implications carefully before they even begin to think about writing. We need to view the meaning of our work from our readers' perspectives and let that permeate the entire paper. An article of 5000 words deserves, as a rule of thumb, at least 500 words devoted to the impact and outcomes of the work. Otherwise, we are just offering our reader something upon which to ruminate, and everyone, particularly our reader, is too busy sifting through too many articles to bother with that.

Before moving on, make notes in answer to some of the questions listed above. Don't worry yet at this stage whether you have exactly the right words. There will be plenty of time to polish your writing. For now, just see if you can identify what really matters about your paper, to whom, and why. As always, it may be a good idea to review these short points with a colleague not completely familiar with your area. Read out your statements of purpose, followed by the key implications of your findings. Do they match? Go through some of the decisions you have made and explain briefly the implications of each. Do they satisfy? Encourage him or her to question you with what are probably the most illuminating words in the scholarly publishing vocabulary – 'So what?'

In the end, you will be delivering the promise of insight and relevant implications you made to your reader who has patiently stayed with you for a few thousand words just to find out. At the very least, you don't wish to frustrate the reader; at best, you want him or her to finish the article knowing that it was of value – and look for your name in future.

In the next chapter we consider how to approach a literature review keeping in mind, of course, that it is not what you have read that will interest anyone else, but what it all means.

Action points

The following exercise will make sure that no one will read your paper and say, 'So what? Now what?' Write a paragraph which sets out, clearly and explicitly, what a practitioner in your field should think about when he or she has finished your paper. Don't shy away from prescribing courses of action; your readers can use their judgement as to whether they want to follow them, ignore them or adapt them. Put yourself in your reader's place for a moment.

Now write another paragraph doing the same for a researcher in your field. You have gained from others by picking up a link of a chain and using it in your research. Make a new link, so the chain can be passed on. Suggest some areas for further research. Remind readers of the limitations and scope of your work.

Congratulations again! Now you have one of your closing paragraphs, with just the bit in the middle to go. Again, keep reviewing your implications section. It is what your readers will take away with them.

5 Making sense of the literature

One question new authors frequently ask is: 'How much of a review of the literature do I need to put in?'. The answer is 'just enough'. The next question, of course, is 'Well, so how much is enough?' for which the answer is again enigmatic, if not totally unhelpful 'It depends'.

There are no rules about how many references a given paper needs: some have only a few, others have hundreds. Editors and reviewers all know how easy it is to add names to a reference list so authors seeking to impress with the length, rather than the relevance, of their list of references are therefore unlikely to do so. Particularly with the accessibility of online databases, bulking a reference list has never been easier, or less meaningful.

An editor or referee seeking to assess the quality of the literature review will formulate two principal questions:

1 Does it reflect the purpose of the paper?
2 What are its implications?

In this chapter we will concentrate on how to ensure that the literature review reflects the purpose and scope, and what you must do to answer the 'so what?' questions. The quantity of the literature review is defined by the original research question, the scope of the paper, and by the author's evaluation of the literature. First, we will examine how the scope affects the choice of literature. Second, we will show how to evaluate it properly to interest and guide the reader.

Scope – how much is enough?

Supporting concepts or evidence in a paper are critically important. The reviewer, and ultimately the reader, needs to know the difference between the author's concept and evidence and those of other contributors to the field. Yet, many authors don't know where to begin or where to stop referring to the work of others. Erring on the side of caution can lead to the absurd, with every idea or concept laboriously referenced to the point that any given paragraph simply reads as a stream of parentheses briefly interrupted by the author's words.

The most important indicator is the paper's scope. Chapters 3 and 4 examined the concept of scope in detail; the nature of scope and how to describe it for the reader should now be familiar concepts. The way you treat the literature – indeed, the very reason why you read it in the first place – is also determined by the scope of the paper and should be clearly stated as such.

Whether you base the paper on a more lengthy piece of work, such as a dissertation, or write it first as a paper, you will have surveyed other relevant works. The criterion influencing how much literature to include in the paper relates to one word: requisite. The reader needs to know, no more nor less, what the key assumptions are. You should therefore provide that knowledge where statements or evidence are questionable or controversial.

If, for example, you are setting out to disprove a strongly held theory, then the reader will want to know exactly whose theory is being disputed. If you want to demonstrate how an accepted theory can be applied in a new setting, then the reader will again want to know what the original theory is. There will often be several tangential issues relating to any theory, and while you may want to follow all those routes in an effort to enlighten the reader completely, you must always ask the following questions:

● Is that requisite knowledge?
● Is it necessary, and does it relate closely to the scope of the paper?

Take, for example, a paper exploring the effects of diet on health. The author, and the reader, will know that many other factors in a person's lifestyle affect health, such as exercise, stress, smoking, genetic predisposition, and so on. It is all too easy for an author who loses his or her focus on the original scope, to follow through the literature on the many other determinants of health. A focused author would allude to the importance of the other factors, but explain that further discussion of them is 'beyond the scope of this paper'.

Continuing with the same example, rather than conduct research on each aspect of diet, the author is likely to have selected a single variable, such as food additives or protein intake, to study. The author has narrowed the scope and must make a statement to that effect. Once again, he or she will not want to enter into a debate on the effects of all dietary influences, but will make reference to one or two key works which have done so. Even within the chosen focus, such as food additives, a balance must be struck between existing research on the issue and the author's own findings. In this case, the author will take care to summarize the current body of knowledge in order to show the reader how he or she has taken it forward. Particularly when the paper is likely to challenge existing theory, the author must ensure that the reader knows that he or she is familiar with the assumed knowledge base. Such care avoids the likelihood of prompting the following reviewer comment:

> Author writes on a subject upon which there has been a lot of debate. It would have been appreciable had he or she demonstrated an awareness of this.

Try to see the scope of the paper as a river, whose banks confine your research. Various tributaries and streams join and issue from the river and connect to related areas that could be followed but lie outside your focus. Identify these for your reader, but resist the temptation to follow them all in your current paper.

Implications of the literature

Work on the assumption that the reviewers reading your paper have read it all before. They are more familiar than are you with the basic great works on the subject. Not only have they read the key writers in the original, they have sifted through hundreds of papers that discuss them. They have probably heard thousands of undergraduates summarize the principal theories and many of their related strands. Indeed, if they read one more treatise about what everybody famous has already said about the subject they would fall asleep.

That you have compiled yet another 'who's who' in the field will not interest your potential reader either. There are, however, occasions when drawing together the literature will have implications for the reader. Two examples in particular will have impact:

1   This is a field in which no one has previously drawn together related thoughts on the subject.
2   This is a field where you alone have discovered that other researchers have got it wrong.

If your paper falls into either of the above two categories, congratulations. Your paper will indeed contribute greatly to the body of knowledge and fire the imagination of your reviewers and readers. Your only problem will be in keeping within your scope and supporting fully your claims that you are truly original. These sorts of papers, which are essentially literature reviews in themselves, are both exceptional and valuable to scholars everywhere.

Summarizing the field, however original the scope, does not eliminate the need to explain the implications. You must still describe what the reader might do next. In most cases, you will accomplish this by indicating the areas for further research, or areas where existing research needs to be re-examined. As a result, you will usefully provide a new framework for an emerging body of knowledge. Students and researchers will benefit from finally having a clear picture of the new field and its antecedents. They will be able to learn from that and build upon it. Although you are not claiming original research, you are making sense for the first time of what has gone before and indicating where researchers might go next.

In the second instance, you may be able to point out why research in a given field may be going in the wrong direction. Many researchers may be working on the assumptions of other researchers that you are now able to point out are wrong. The flaws in the existing body of knowledge are exposed, and you are helping other researchers by leading them away from blind alleys. In that case, you must take pains to explain the key points which are being criticized. More than ever, you must retain full attention on the scope. An author who is starkly refuting existing theories will be subject to close scrutiny by reviewers and readers, some of whom may want to defend the theories in question and will look for any reason, however small, to discredit him or her. Moving away from the point may reveal weaknesses on related topics to use against the author, even if they are not entirely relevant. The message here is: hold your ground and resist the temptation to wander! Everything else must be eliminated using 'Occam's razor'.

Occam's razor

The principle of Occam's razor derives from the thirteenth-century Franciscan monk, William of Occam, whose philosophical work was later developed by John Locke into positivism. Apart from his memorable plea to Louis of Bavaria for protection – 'Do thou defend me by the sword, and I will defend thee with my pen' – Occam is known for his principle that a universal concept is only an abstract idea. He urged people to slash away everything that is abstract, keeping hypotheses to a minimum. An abstract idea, he reasoned, only exists in our minds, therefore does not exist empirically, therefore does not exist at all. By evoking Occam's razor we are cutting away all but the essential, to a certain extent simplifying our work, but to a larger extent ensuring that we do not become embroiled with too many other hypotheses or points of view simultaneously, and which we are therefore less able to defend.

William of Occam has become an unlikely guru to several practitioners and writers in the field of quality management (Pirsig and 1974 and Duffin, 1995, for example). The notion of cutting away the extraneous to seek the simplest and most direct solution is one which appeals to many wrestling with quality assurance in organizations. Quality and reliability equal simplicity; the fewer steps in a process or argument, the more likely it is to deliver what it should. Don't make the mistake of confusing quality with complexity. If in doubt, sharpen the razor, and shave away the non-essential.

Evaluate – don't regurgitate

Other than the examples noted above, most authors will be using the literature to help the reader understand the context of their research. As explained earlier, you should strenuously avoid behaving like a third-year student writing an essay on what everyone else has said. Many reviewers look first at the list of references to assess quickly whether the author is drawing upon recent, or previously neglected, authors. A reference list with all the usual names from earlier decades will tell the reviewer immediately that the author is simply rehashing the obvious. In most cases, this would disqualify it as a publishable paper in a reputable journal – the reviewer's only conceivable reaction can be 'So what?'.

As a consistent rule of thumb, check your own references for a balance between old and new. Ask yourself if you have explored fully the implications of original or seminal works, or are you reporting on them parrot-fashion? Before taking for granted that the theories still stand, have you used a citation index to track what more recent authors are saying about the standard theories? There's little point in blithely referring to the well accepted theories of 'Professor So-and-so' if, during the last year, recent research has invalidated her work. As ever, the original scope will dictate how extensively you need to report on the work of other researchers.

Apart from simply tacking on a few references to support the key points, authors must be able to evaluate the literature. Editors send many articles back because the author was unable to move beyond merely describing what he or she had read. Such a paper caused one reviewer to comment:

> This paper reads more like an undergraduate essay than a serious article for an academic/professional journal. It is not based on any original research and contributes virtually nothing new to our understanding about EDI. Although it reviews quite a large literature, most of the works receive only a very superficial mention. There is little attempt to integrate or critically evaluate earlier published work on the subject.

What can we learn about the reviewer's exhortation to integrate and critically evaluate earlier published works? Many supervisors, myself included, direct their students to follow several steps when conducting an evaluative literature review. This, eventually, helps the student realize that a review itself is only a first step. The sequence I devised to help students remember how to evaluate is:

Summarize → synthesize → analyse → authorize

Summarize

This is just the first step in a literature review but is also, unfortunately, where most people stop. Who are the key contributors to the field of enquiry and what did they individually say of significance? As readers will note, answering this question is impossible if our scope is as yet ill-defined or we have allowed ourselves to drift away from it. Whether or not we want to summarize each author or move straight on to the next step depends on both the scope and the audience. Are we attempting to pull apart contributions made thus far so that we may criticize them? In that case, we will have to summarize the key findings of each person first. If, however, we are trying to provide a quick overview of past work so that our readers can now see our findings in context it will be more important to synthesize rather than summarize.

Synthesize

Following a summary of key concepts, we need to draw out the implications for our reader by making sense of where the past has brought us. We might choose to synthesize using a chronological model that shows how one person's theory was enriched by the next person, before another person later extended it, and so on. Or, we might synthesize according to a key theme we are investigating.

Read the following example about occupational stress in the ambulance service, published in the *Journal of Managerial Psychology*. After a two-paragraph introduction, the authors write:

> With specific regard to the health service, Payne and Firth-Cozens (2) argued that the nature of the work carried out by health workers renders them particularly susceptible to stress-related illnesses. Cooper and Rees (3) looked at occupational stress across a broad range of occupational groups within the health service. However, their study did not include ambulance service workers, who not only are primary health workers but also operate as an emergency service.
>
> What little research has been carried out into health and well-being within the ambulance service has been based on the explicit assumption that such work is inherently stressful. This has led authors such as Sparius (4), Thompson and Suzuki (5), James and Wright (6) and James (7) to focus their approach on the identification of possible sources of stress and their relationship with a series of moderator variables. In a call for further research, James (7) observes an apparent paradox, that ambulance work is stressful but rewarding.
>
> The purpose of the present study is to undertake a diagnostic investigation of work stress in the ambulance service in a systematic manner which allows stress outcomes to be measured and compared with other occupational groups. In this instance stress outcomes in the ambulance service are compared with those of the fire service. (Young and Cooper, 1995)

While experts on neither stress nor the ambulance service, we can certainly tell from those few paragraphs where the state of knowledge has brought us, where it should be leading and what the authors intend to do about it.

Analyse

Through analysis, the author critically evaluates previous work. At that time, he or she will be highlighting contributions or flaws influencing his or her own research, if not the body of knowledge as a whole. The scope for the evaluation is the question being pursued and the author's findings relating to it. This step can only follow the previous two steps. Literature cannot be analysed without first summarizing key stages in its evolution and making sense of, or synthesizing its current position.

Authorize

At some point in the paper the author will describe his or her own findings in light of the critical evaluation of the literature. The authorization may be in support of previous works or it may be authorizing the author's own view opposing the literature thus far. This is a final and critical stage of the paper, for having looked at the literature, made sense of it and analysed it, the author must either extend the body of knowledge or purposefully depart from it.

When authors fail to put their stamp on the body of knowledge, the reviewers mutter, 'So what? Here you have described where everyone else is, told me what you have done, yet not made any connection between the two'. It is the moment of connection between the published past and the present that gives the reader the whole picture of the author's work. It is the final and most conclusive implication an author can share, yet it is one which many authors resist, for reasons discussed in previous chapters.

Summary

We have considered so far that authors are frequently criticized for not treating the literature in ways that are relevant to the question or helpful in providing insight to the body of knowledge. Of course, researchers normally rectify these problems during the course of academic research. Righting the wrongs will take more than revising a paper. If the core literature review is weak, it will be impossible to hide the flaws simply by writing well. What concerns us here is how to treat a good literature review for the purpose of communicating the salient points to the readers.

You must therefore pay attention to the need to be:

- thorough
- relevant
- critical.

Being thorough means that you have read and evaluated the literature influencing the question and is one of the factors which most affects the quality of articles. It is not possible to be thorough if you are not sure what the question is; this explains the weaknesses of many papers.

Many authors frustrate their own efforts by allowing themselves to drift off on irrelevant tangents. Once again, being clear about the purpose and the implications eliminate this problem before it can start. The length of academic papers range between 3500 and 12000 words. Economy is therefore necessary if we are to retain the reviewer's, let alone the reader's, attention.

Try to imagine the background of the editor, reviewer and the reader. Remember, many will be as familiar with the classic literature as you are. Their purpose in reading your paper is not to be reminded yet again about what everyone they have ever read has said before. They want to know what you are doing with what's been said.

Failure to critically evaluate the literature is a frequent criticism voiced by reviewers and by research student supervisors. If we apply the 'so what?' question here we can find that much of what we've been busy writing is not review but regurgitation.

For the last five chapters we have explored the paper from the author's point of view, reminding ourselves about why we should publish, and why sometimes we feel we shouldn't. On making a closer analysis of quality criteria, we have found that even good research is not communicated if the paper has no purpose or implications. Next, we will be turning the mirror round and reflecting the world of the editor, reviewer and reader. What we will see is a different point of view entirely. For many aspiring or new authors it will be an unfamiliar world, a place of mystery and arcane knowledge. And yet, the reality is very different. Editors, reviewers and readers are not, after all, formidable or forbidding. They're just people like you.

Action points

Note down the key reference sources in your paper. Next to each one, make a short note about why you are referencing it. What value does it add? Look at the publication dates. How many are more than five years old? How many are less than two years old?

Now, draft a few paragraphs dealing with one of the aspects of the literature you are reviewing. Don't spend much time polishing them – just put them down in draft form. Check whether you have summarized (briefly captured the relevant key points of each of your cited authorities), synthesized (brought together any threads), analysed (brought the section to a relevant and logical conclusion) and authorized (put your own stamp upon it).

PART II

Think 'audience'

6 Communicating quality

We all suffer from self-delusion. That is one of the qualities which separates us from animals and from gods. Humans are capable of tricking not only each other but also themselves. One of our delusions may be that we are the most interesting person in the world. Another, and perhaps a more tragic one, is that we are the least interesting. Somewhere in between, in the grey area of compromise, lies the truth. The author's job is to balance what he or she thinks is important against what other people think is important.

Being a writer doesn't mean that our sole objective is merely to please an audience. Part of the fun of being a writer is that we can please ourselves a little, and that sometimes we can challenge, outwit, tease and even annoy our target audience. But unless we are able to communicate with that audience, we are not in the game at all. Sometimes, that means taking different stances for different groups, or altering the tone and style of what we write. A compromise, maybe, but it isn't any less worthwhile for that.

The kind of approach which includes our needs and the needs of other people is known as market- or customer-orientation. We expect lawyers or accountants to satisfy our professional service needs. We expect people in the service industry to satisfy our needs, be that in a hotel or a restaurant. Editors, reviewers and readers expect authors to satisfy their needs. In this case, the author is the manufacturer of a product which may be distributed either electronically or on paper. The person who receives it is not there to manage the author's ego or ambitions, but rather to find their own needs satisfied and sometimes the needs of other people whom they serve.

In this chapter, and the next two, we will investigate the nature of the relationship between authors, editors, reviewers, readers, publishers and intermediaries such as librarians. The objective is to help authors see the world from another point of view, most specifically from the point of view of their customers. Although each customer, or journal, is different, this chapter discusses a quality assessment exercise which revealed some important distinctions and shared characteristics amongst the journals surveyed. From this we can deduce that the author's job is to satisfy the criteria of a target audience.

The more the author can understand the needs of other people in the publishing process, the easier it becomes to create articles acceptable to their purposes. It also becomes easier for the author to take constructive criticism and work with it, rather than see it as a personal slight. We will, therefore, explore this theme in more depth before moving on to the mechanics of getting it right in writing.

Think 'customer'

It is for the reasons above that I unabashedly speak of the editors, reviewers and readers as 'customers'. Strictly speaking, the editorial board is the customer and the reader the consumer. This is a distinction felt in other areas of our lives with which we are perhaps more familiar. People shopping in a supermarket on behalf of their family are customers; the family is the consumer, or eventual end-user of the goods purchased. The manufacturer and retailer have to satisfy and appeal to both groups in subtly different ways, as an adult viewing the advertisements during children's programmes quickly discovers. Food manufacturers have supermarkets as their customer, and buyers and users of their produce as consumers. In the same way, the author must satisfy the needs of the editorial team which are aligned to, but subtly different from, the needs of the readers.

Authors must recognize that they create and deliver a product (article) for not only their own personal satisfaction but for the needs of their customers and consumers. If the product they create is not what the customer wants, it will be returned. If the product is not delivered in the manner which the customer expects, it will not be so highly regarded. Finally, the customer will decide whether or not he or she wants to continue to 'do business' with the author in the future. So, too, will the consumer.

It is the notion of relationship publishing, suggested to me by Professor Richard Teare, editor of *The International Journal of Contemporary Hospitality Management*, that new authors will often consider for the first time. There are a limited number of journals reflecting the author's own subject area. Over time, those journals will probably become the chosen outlet for the author. If the product being delivered to the customer meets the customer's needs consistently (and the needs of their customers), it is only natural that the customer will think more favourably about the supplier who accomplishes it.

That doesn't, or shouldn't, mean that the author's work is accepted without due review, but it does mean that the author may be considered by an editor looking for specific papers on a specific subject. As a result, the author may be invited, as a reliable supplier, to contribute future papers, or asked to review books or even other papers.

If the author delivers what the reader expects and wants, then the satisfied consumer will look for the author's name in the future and be more favourably disposed to journals which publish the author's work. That, in turn, benefits the journal and, by virtue of the journal's reputation, the editor and editorial review board. Everyone wants to be associated with success; authors can help make that happen not only for themselves, but for others too.

By considering the relationship in its entirety we are accepting the notion of a continuing partnership – one which is not based on single transactions, but one which builds over time into a mutually rewarding experience. As Teare says, 'The author, the editor, the publisher and the reader share an interest in the value and quality of the product which they jointly create and consume. The stakeholders are dependent on each other and the relationships are "successful" when their interests overlap.' Figure 6.1 illustrates this concept.

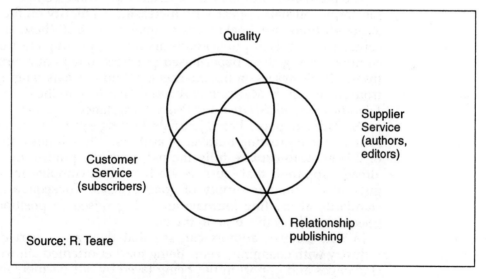

Figure 6.1:   Success through relationship publishing

The supply chain

Many authors picture themselves outside the publishing process rather than being an integral part of it. Academic publishing is an unusual example of a customer–supplier relationship because the suppliers – the authors – are the same sort of people, and quite often the very same people, who are the readers, or consumers. We tend to read the journals we write for, and are able to evaluate articles against the needs we have at the time. Although this should make it easier for us to put ourselves in the place of others in the relationship, as we will examine in the following chapters, it often does not in practice. We are frequently bound by the same problems which plague many manufacturers, that of being product-oriented.

Product orientation leads producers to become absorbed only in the interest they have in the product itself, not in the needs of those serviced by the products. If we look at examples from other industries, we can see what problems are created. IBM, for instance, was known as a very successful producer of computers. They encountered problems when customers became less interested in the proprietor's name on the computer and sought more satisfaction from software applications. The American car industry was successfully producing large, fuel-intensive vehicles until consumers began to demand more fuel-efficient cars in the early 1970s. That gave an opening for the Japanese producers who moved into the market with smaller, more economical models. Interestingly, they would not have been able to move quite so quickly had they not already anticipated the changing needs of the market.

The publishing industry is experiencing similar competitive pressures. Electronic journals appear with increasing regularity on the Internet, and although there are weaknesses of quality control, these are being overcome. Thousands of publications are now appearing electronically, some complementing their paper-based partners, others appearing only electronically. Browsers on the Internet can find journals ranging in diversity from *Acropolis: the Magazine of Acrobat Publishing* to the *Canadian Journal of Educational Administration and Policy*. Simultaneously, there is a continuing proliferation of paper-based journals, leaving a growing number of choices available to a growing number of authors. While it lies outside the scope of this book to explore fully the nature of the publishing industry, it is already apparent that journals are having to compete more strongly to guarantee a regular supply of good articles. Consequently, the quality standards of existing journals are being raised to position them more unequivocally as the 'best' in the field.

In that context, authors can see that they are a part of a changing industry with changing needs. Being market-oriented allows us to see the challenges and opportunities being faced by our partners in the relationship and will hopefully make it easier for us to adapt our method or style to meet those needs. Recognizing that we are part of the whole process, not separate from it, can lead us to appreciate the dynamics of the give-and-take upon which any relationship is based.

The exchange process

Most interactions between individuals or organizations involve an exchange. Sometimes, the exchange may be money-for-labour, as in a job, but in most cases it is not so obvious or mechanistic. The police service, for example, operates successfully only if there is an exchange between them and the general public. The police will exchange protection and fair dealing in return for the public's respect, reasonable behaviour and taxes. Students attending university exchange their time, money and respect for lecturers for the lecturers' commitment, the university's quality control procedures and, if all goes well, a recognized qualification.

Think this through from the perspective of those handling an author's work. Editors and reviewers, as we shall see in Chapter 7, exchange their time, reputation and intellect in return for a quality article offered by an author. Readers exchange time, and often subscription money, for an article which satisfies their own quality criteria. The arrangement is freely made on both sides and has to be reciprocal to work. Just as the police service would break down if the general public refused to comply, so the author–editor–reader relationship would break down if one of its members decided not to reciprocate.

Some, often unpublished, authors complain that editors don't understand them, or say that if readers of their research can't get the point, that's the reader's problem not theirs. They resist changing their precious work in the belief that to do so would lower their standards. It is interesting, at this point, to question why they suppose that their standards are an absolute criterion of quality. Perhaps they are right; perhaps they are wrong. But unless you have an already vast reputation, this kind of uncompromising, self-absorbed view of your work is likely to ensure that you remain largely unheard. When we are self-indulgent seventeen-year-olds we can quote Thomas Gray ('Full many a flower is born to blush unseen, And waste its sweetness on the desert air') when we feel that no one really understands us. But, as adults, we should try to put aside teenage indulgences in favour of an appropriate degree of pragmatism.

Communication is a two-way process, involving a transmitter and a receiver, much like a radio. If both aren't tuned into the same frequency, the message will be garbled, or not heard at all. The transmitter's job is to understand which frequency the receiver is tuned into. Anything written for publication must be read eventually by someone, somewhere. If we are to understand how to adjust the tuning, we must first understand who the receivers are. Consider how easy it is to misunderstand each other in our daily lives, simply because different words will have different meanings to other people. One person's terrorist is another person's freedom fighter. Or, as someone once said, 'I know you know what you think I said, but what you think I said is not what I meant'. It is the author's job, not the reader's, to understand those nuances.

A word which is increasingly used by authors is 'quality': the need to write 'quality' articles for 'quality' journals. Quality can be a misunderstood concept, and is often used as a halfhearted excuse not to accept rejection or requests for revision. It is necessary to define what is meant by quality and how we know it when we see it.

Quality counts

Years ago, a judge presiding over an obscenity trial became impatient with the defending lawyer's attempts to define what obscenity actually was. Finally, in a moment of exasperation, the judge bellowed: 'I can't define it and you can't define it, but we both know what it is when we see it!' Quality, it seems, falls into that category. We may not be able to agree on a definition of it, yet we all know it when we see it. Refereed journals are the bastions of quality in a given field. They have set themselves up to select only those articles which meet the journal's objectives and the standards within the field. The standards are not set by the journal alone; they reflect standards within the community that the journal serves. In other words, they reflect the quality standards demanded by the customers.

And yet, we ask, what is quality? 'Fitness for the purpose intended', as the consumer protection laws state? Adherence to an absolute norm set by a professional body? Of course, it may be those things and more, but ultimately it is whatever the customer says it is.

In 1993 and 1994, the Buckingham Consortium, of which I am a director, conducted research on behalf of academic journal publishers MCB University Press into the nature of quality in academic publishing. The research was commissioned by MCB because they were seeking to understand how their own journals rated against other leading journals in the field. Not only did we discover and refine a list of seven determinants of quality in an academic paper, we also discovered that the relative importance of that list varied from journal to journal. Different customers were demanding something unique each time. The only exception to this exclusivity was the referees' feedback to authors. There we discovered the common standards of purpose and implications which have been discussed in previous chapters.

The question of how to measure and judge the quality of an academic publication is one with which every acquisitions librarian is painfully familiar. The formula of functionality (how well does it do what it's supposed to do?) plus features (what additional things does it do?), plus price (how much does it cost?) might work for a computer system in the library, or for shelving in the library – but does it work for journals in the library?

A common quality indicator is the number of citations of an article or journal in other articles, which is readily measurable but flawed, in that it is biased heavily towards high circulation journals. It's hard to argue with popularity, but popularity and quality do not always correlate. It is certainly a problem in a very narrow or new field.

The functionality, features and price formula is, actually, a reliable and robust one. But, just as for shelving and computers, value-adding functionality and features in academic publishing need to be uncovered, and the higher-value ones differentiated from the lower-value ones. This technique of distinguishing between a multitude of variables, and assigning a value to them, was first explored in the 1970s by Green and Wind using an approach called conjoint analysis (see Green and Wind, 1975).

The 1994 Buckingham Consortium Survey into quality in academic journals

It was this technique that provided the basic analytical framework for the 1994 Buckingham Consortium Survey. Simply stated, conjoint analysis asks for weighting (how important, relatively, is a factor?) and ranking (how well do we and our competitors perform in delivering it?). The important factor, is, of course, to concentrate on doing the right things well.

A pilot survey directed to editors, editorial advisers and authors was first conducted to test out concepts of quality criteria. This uncovered 14 separate quality indicators, clustered under three broad headings:

- prestige and reputation of editor, advisers and authors
- quality and content of articles
- presentation.

The survey isolated, to some extent, people's perception of features and functions of an article in a journal, which led to perceptions of quality.

The full survey was then taken from a random sample of contributors to, and consumers of, ten reviewed, mature journals – 1000 in all. Each journal was benchmarked against those closest to it in its particular field. The data were then analysed using weightings and rankings. Respondents were asked how a journal performed on each criterion, on a scale of 1–5 and what was the relative importance of each criterion within the broad criteria groupings of prestige, content and presentation. Respondents were also asked to rate the importance of each criteria grouping as high, medium or low. In that way, conclusions could be drawn about possible quality indicators, and a possible 'prescription' drawn up on how to improve quality by strengthening those indicators which would make the most impact.

The 14 criteria, in their three groupings, were:

1   The prestige and reputation of people involved with a journal in both writing and selection of articles.

- Prestige of author(s)
- Prestige of editor(s)
- Prestige of editorial advisory board members.

2   The content of a journal and of the articles within it.

- The practical applications which can be drawn from articles – does the journal favour practicality and pragmatism?
- Its originality of findings and approach – does the journal favour new and original work and approaches?
- Its clarity and readability – does the journal favour articles which are written for ease of reading?
- The rigour of research methodology employed – does the journal favour articles which have demonstrable rigour to their conclusions and findings
- Its contribution to the appropriate body of knowledge – does the journal favour articles which make a significant impact on their selected field?
- Its mix of features and subject matter coverage – does the journal favour a wide-ranging approach which includes reviews, news, editorial comment and so on?
- Its internationality – does the journal favour articles which draw on international perspectives?

3   Presentation. How does a journal look? How appropriate is its appearance to its content? How well does the presentational form facilitate the message?

- Cover
- Typography and layout
- Ease of reference (contents page, page numbers, indexing and so on)
- Use of graphics and pictures

The findings showed that:

- Content was most important, as a whole category, followed by prestige, followed by presentation.
- The prestige of authors in the journal was in all cases more important than the prestige of the editor and advisory board which were normally about equal.
- The relative importance of content factors varied with the type of journal. The mix of features was always least important, preceded by internationality.
- How 'academic' a journal was perceived to be was apparently the determining factor of importance ratings:

  - very academic: research rigour, followed by impact on the body of knowledge
  - academic: impact on the body of knowledge followed by research rigour

- theory/practice balance: body of knowledge impact followed by practical applications
- practice orientation: practical applications, followed by impact on the body of knowledge

- Originality was a consistently important factor in all types of journal.
- Ease of reference, and typography and layout, were most important in determining quality of presentation.

We will examine closely in Chapter 10 what each of those criteria means to authors, and how they can be met. For now, it is important to realize that, other than the common requirement for explicit implications, quality is determined by the particular journal.

Summary

This chapter is intended to help you view the members of a publishing relationship both as customers and consumers who, with the author, form a relationship. The relationship is voluntary on all sides, but the perspectives of those involved will change depending on the point of view. Building an idea of what is required, based on the customer's and consumer's viewpoints, can help an author create work which is more likely to be acceptable.

Finally, even quality is an arbitrary notion depending upon who is defining it. Our market-oriented approach inevitably leads us to conclude that it will be defined by the customer. Our next step, therefore, is to work out how we can find out more about who the customers and consumers are, what they need, and how we can deliver it.

Action points

Find two journals which you consider to be 'quality' publications. Note, using the framework set out in this chapter, what it is about the journals that give them their 'quality'. What factors are most important, and what factors are less so? Note any differences between the two.

Now carry out the same exercise with two or three articles which have impressed you recently. Where does their 'quality' come from? What does it comprise? Again, note any differences.

Taking a little time and care over this exercise will put you further ahead than most authors in understanding the mechanics of quality in learned publishing. And once you understand the mechanics, you can go on to build some of them into your own work.

7 Who are the editors and reviewers?

If you were asked to sit down right now and write a letter, you would surely ask three obvious questions: to whom, about what, and why? We are all pestered almost daily with unsolicited communications from people wanting us to buy a new product or, at the very least, enter our name to win a massive prize for which we have supposedly been shortlisted. Most people don't like those kinds of communications and refer to them as junk mail.

But suppose you received a letter from your local supermarket, thanking you for using their loyalty card and informing you that the next time you do your shopping the manager will personally present you with two free bottles of the Californian wine you usually buy. Would you accept that offer? Very likely. That's the difference between junk mail and well targeted mail. One is a blanket communication paying no respect to the person receiving it and the other is created with the person's own preferences and habits in mind. We have all experienced both kinds of communication and know to which we respond the best.

Why is it then that so many authors send editors junk mail? As we will investigate thoroughly in Chapter 9, editors reject up to half the articles they receive simply because they are not suited to that particular journal's brief. Editors are inundated with inappropriate articles on subjects outside the scope of the journal, or articles written in a style clearly unsuitable for that journal's audience.

In this chapter and the next, we will penetrate the journal to become acquainted with those who have its success most at heart – editors, reviewers, publishers and readers. The objective is to create a mental picture of real people, just like you, trying to do their jobs in the best and least difficult way possible. These chapters are about how to make their, and your, job easier.

Whenever you are writing for publication, you are trying to convey your ideas and evidence to another person. As with most publishing, scholarly publishing relies on several layers of people to help your work reach the final reader in the best shape possible. Each layer is populated with individuals who have slightly different needs and standards. You need to satisfy them all.

Your link in the chain

As described in the previous chapters, authors are involved in a publishing process composed of several different people seeking different benefits. Think of the publishing process as a supply chain. At the head of the chain is the manufacturer, the person who makes the product. In this case, the product is a paper destined for an academic journal, and the manufacturer is you.

You could simply photocopy your paper and send it to your friends, but this is insufficient to help you reach a wider, unfamiliar, audience. Fortunately, there are distributors whose job it is to package your article into a journal with other articles, let people know it's available, deliver it to those who have ordered it, and collect money to pay for all their activities. The distributor, in this sense, is the publisher.

That could be the end of the story, but a few questions arise. How will the distributor decide what articles to publish? How will the distributor keep up with the changing state-of-the-art? The distributor appoints an expert to read the articles first and select those which deserve publication. This person is usually called an editor.

This, again, could be the end of the story and often is for the less academic and more practice-based journals. But now much more is hanging in the balance. Institutions are rating academics on their publication record, and the institutions themselves are being rated by others. Someone has to be sure that the best decisions are being made. What if the single editor doesn't know everything about every variation in the field? What if their best friend is the author? How will the distributor and the editor know that decisions are being made fairly and by the most informed minds? They appoint a team to help the editor called the review board. Normally, publication in a reviewed (or refereed – the terms are used synonymously) journal counts for more than publication in an unreviewed, or editor-only reviewed journal.

Now, between the manufacturer and final publication, we already have three links in the chain: publisher, editor and review board. But, as with most learned journals, readers usually gain access through a library. The librarian is therefore another intermediary between manufacturer and reader, making four links. The librarian may be informed by another intermediary known as an agent who will often handle all the billing requirements. If the article is being distributed electronically, we can replace 'library' with Internet. Finally, the reader will have the paper available to him or her.

Each person involved in the chain has compatible, but slightly different, needs and pressures. Each will approach the paper and individual journal with slightly different questions.

Author: 'Can I get my paper accepted in this journal?'
Editor: 'Does it meet the aims of the journal and its audience?'
Review board: 'Is it the right quality?'
Publisher: 'Is the journal performing to market expectations?'
Librarian: 'How can I give access to it – direct, interlibrary loan or online?'
Reader: 'Where can I read it? Is it useful to me?'

The supply chain remains much the same for electronic communication. Whether the final output is paper-based or electronic, it must still be distributed around a network, it must still be reviewed if it is to count towards a publication record, and it must still be accessible to the reader. Authors can always go direct to reader, through the post or through a modem. But that, alone, will not presume quality control, and it is the presumption of quality control which makes a refereed journal and the papers within it significant.

Each member of this supply chain has a need to fulfil. If each member of the chain understands the others' needs, they are more likely to be able to satisfy them. Once each member has done that once, and learned what they need, they can then move towards building a relationship with the other members of the chain. As an author, you might find you can publish regularly in the same journal or even another journal published by the same distributor. This brings you to the ultimate goal: how to repeat the performance, and possibly, if desired, move towards reviewing and editing yourself. And, if that seems too ambitious, remember that we are all part of the same community, although we play different parts in the whole. Academic publishers, editors and reviewers aren't strangers, they're people like you.

Let's now investigate these people, what they need, and why they lose sleep at night.

Understanding editors

Editors are busy people – always and by definition. No publisher will appoint an editor who is out of touch with the field or has no reputation amongst his or her peers. Editors are respected within their institutions and their academic community. They are not, typically, has-beens who retire to the south of France with only a few journal papers to look over before lunch. Publishers are not interested in people who have left the network. Editors are extremely active, time-pressured people constantly involved in teaching, researching, writing and editing.

Any academic, and even some students, appreciate that an academic's life is not always an easy one. There are classes to teach, papers to mark, students to supervise, committees to appear on, conferences to attend, papers to write ... and then on top of that load the editor will elect to take responsibility for a journal. Spare a few moments to consider exactly what that task entails.

Editing a journal will, during an average year, involve hundreds of extra hours of work. Included in the editor's remit is: advising the publisher on the direction of the journal; agreeing editorial strategy; appointing a review board; monitoring the workings of the review board to ensure quality and timeliness; accepting articles for the review process; corresponding with reviewers; taking their feedback and passing it on to the author; seeing the paper through one or several revisions; making sure all the documentation is in order; selecting which issue the paper should appear in based on pagination requirements and editorial balance; sending it to the publisher in time for the agreed production schedule; looking over the proofs; answering queries from sub-editors; and finally sending the approved version back to the publisher on schedule. The last thing they need is junk mail.

Now that we have put ourselves in the editor's place and appreciated the demands placed on him or her, we might reasonably ask, why bother? What do editors get out of it?

'It's an opportunity to read research at the cutting edge,' says Professor David Carson who edits the *European Journal of Marketing*. David is also author of some 30 published papers and a leading academic based at the University of Ulster. Being the first person to look at a paper sent to one of the world's most respected marketing journals gives him a privileged position of insight. Keeping ahead of the game is an important benefit of being an editor.

Professor David Bennett, at Aston University, who edits *Integrated Manufacturing Systems*, agrees that keeping ahead is important, but so also is keeping in touch. He appreciates the networking benefits of being an editor; his contact with many hundreds of authors worldwide extends his participation in the international arena. He has already published 11 refereed papers, plus editorials and books, and finds his job increasingly enriched by the growing numbers of people he is getting to know.

Scratch the surface a little, and most editors will admit they experience a thrill from helping new authors along. Beneath the austere image of the respected professor lurks someone who hasn't forgotten the fun of teaching and hasn't forgotten what it's like to be a novice.

Professor Harry Dickinson, editor of *History*, says he edits a journal because 'I believe it is important to the health of the subject, to the practitioners of the subject and to students of the subject of history that good work is published. I am anxious to promote the careers of new scholars as well as seeking good work from established scholars.'

And then, of course, there is the personal benefit gained from being an editor. It looks good on the CV and it's good for the institution. Editors are invited to speak at conferences, contribute chapters to books, edit special editions and comment on topical issues in the news. In short, they gain kudos. Set against the work and commitment they put into it, it's a fair reward. But some authors make it more worthwhile than others.

One benefit editors don't usually receive is financial. Academic editors typically do not receive a salary like editors of magazines or newspapers. Most are paid an annual or per issue 'honorarium' to help defray the expenses of administrative support, telephone and postage. Were they paid what they are worth per hour, publishers could not afford them.

For an editor, some authors are good news, and some not so good. Some make their lives easier and some make them wonder if they should give up editing and let someone else have all the headaches. The best are welcomed not only because their worthwhile papers improve the journal's, and therefore the editor's, stature but because their professionalism smoothes the flow.

Here is how authors can make life hard for editors.

Poor targeting

We'll discuss this in more detail in Chapter 9, but remember that editors often say that the most common cause for outright rejection, before entering the review process, is that the paper is simply not suited to the journal. Maybe the journal is highly theoretical and your paper concentrates on a single practical application, or vice versa. Perhaps the journal is devoted to a single branch of a discipline and your paper is too broad-based. Fitting your work to the right place is a first, important step.

Receiving an article which is not in tune with the editorial aims of the journal is a disappointment, akin to the feeling experienced by one poor fellow who opened his post one day to find an offer describing how to enter a free draw, the prize for which was a year's free service by a garden maintenance company, a free lawnmower and a lifetime supply of weed-killer – a pity the letter was addressed to his home, apartment 26, floor eight! Right from the start, the sender of a mistargeted communication is saying: 'See whether you like it or not. I couldn't be bothered to find out first whether you might be interested.'

Poor communication

Some authors, fortunate enough to see their papers pass into the review stream, then convey their indifference to the editor. The reviewers decide that the paper has potential and suggest a few revisions that the editor sends on to the author who doesn't even acknowledge the letter. The editor or sub-editor has a query about a reference or the heading for a table and, again, the author doesn't reply or replies three months later. To the editor that garden in the south of France now begins to seem quite appealing.

Multiple submissions

An editor who considers a paper for publication may rightly be accused of being a naive, innocent, even overtrusting sort of person. Strangely, perhaps, the editor usually believes that the author has behaved responsibly and taken note not only of the general ethics of the academic community but also of the words printed in black and white, in very clear language, on the Notes for Authors in most journals. This is where editors explain that they only want to see papers that have not been submitted to other journals. But, once in a while, an author ignores that, only to inform the editor a few months later, after the article has gone through the review process, that, regrettably, it has just been accepted elsewhere.

Rewriting at proof stage

Most publishers still send authors proofs of their paper before publication. We will discuss later on how to handle proofs, but the point we want to make here is to resist the temptation to rewrite. Many publishers actually charge authors who make changes to anything other than a typesetting error at proof stage. When authors want to add a few sentences here and there just to improve things a little, it generates only delays and frustration to everyone concerned.

If the above examples demonstrate how authors make life difficult for editors, what can they do to make it better?

Send the right paper to the right journal

- Understand the aims of the journal.
- Conform to specifications given in the Notes for Authors.
- Refer when appropriate to other papers in the same journal.

Keep in touch

- Acknowledge everything immediately.
- Respond promptly with requests for revision, corrections and so on.

Assist with administration

- Keep to deadlines.
- Complete all documentation fully and promptly.
- Supply finished paper and disk precisely to specification.
- Don't amend proofs, other than printer's errors.

Doing all the above can ease an acceptable paper through the process and help build a positive relationship with the editor. Moving on to the next link in the chain, what can authors do to understand the reviewers and make their jobs easier?

Understanding reviewers

Because editors have a name, and sometimes a face, put to the journal we are more likely to picture them as real people. Reviewers, however, are expected to remain anonymous. Who are these mysterious arbiters of quality? People like you, people you know, professors at your own university, someone you saw present a paper at a conference. Nobody mysterious, nobody forbidding. After all, the proper term for the process is 'peer review'. A peer is someone who is your equal.

The benefits they derive from their work are similar to the benefits experienced by editors. They keep up to date in their own fields, they keep in touch with who is writing interesting papers based on original thought or research and they improve their own reputation by being associated with a good-quality journal. That doesn't mean it's an easy job, and any remuneration they receive is paltry in comparison to the commitment, intellectual insight and time that they give. Usually it's a subscription to the journal, and the occasional 'thank you' note or Christmas card from the editor or publisher.

Reviewers might read anything from one or two papers a year to several papers each month. They read each carefully and in great detail so that they can send constructive comments back. Some journals supply reviewers with a form to draw their attention to the specific quality criteria being sought and to help the reviewer respond in a methodical fashion. An example appears in the Appendix.

The review process is normally a 'blind' one. That means the editor knows who the author is and to which reviewers he or she is sending the paper, but authors don't know who is reviewing it. Reviewers don't know who the author is because the editor has removed the author's name and affiliation from the front of the paper. Why? Just to make sure that everyone is playing fair, that the reviewer is not easing the path of someone because he or she knows them, and that he or she isn't overawed by someone with a towering reputation in their field. In many cases, the editor will send a paper to two 'blind' reviewers, and collate both comments before giving feedback to the author. Some journals review every paper published four times. If ever you've wondered what 'blind reviewed', 'double-blind reviewed' or 'quadruple-blind reviewed' means on a journal's Notes for Authors page, that's what it means.

Editors will normally send a reviewer papers that reflect that individual's own subject knowledge, expertise and interest. The author can therefore assume that the paper is being read by someone who is not only a recognized leader in the field, but someone who reads papers similar to the author's regularly and thoroughly. They can also assume that they don't have two heads, green fangs or put their socks on much differently to anyone else!

What can you expect to hear from them? How are they likely to give their comments? In words like these:

> To increase the value of the paper, I recommend that the authors go back a step or two to show how the attributes are selected, rated and then analysed to achieve the final equivalent-value prices. The subject matter is very interesting and the cited examples are very relevant to the services industry.

Now, that's not so bad. There's something you can work with, delivered in a tone which doesn't send you scurrying away, deflated and demoralized. That is what you should, and can, expect from the better journals. Unfortunately, not all reviewers provide feedback in such constructive tones. Normally, the better editors don't approve of callous criticism any more than authors do and diplomatically filter out terse review comments. But, if you do receive such a comment, just swallow hard, analyse what is being asked of you and start work on the revisions.

When we conducted our survey of referees' reports, we asked editors of 20 journals to send us five reports 'at random'. Two editors deliberately chose reports from different reviewers on the same paper to demonstrate that reviewers themselves sometimes don't agree. That's understandable, when you think about it. Reviewers will each have a slightly different perspective on what's important in the subject area and will themselves be at different stages in their thinking. No one claims that reviewers are perfect or even unanimous. An editor is not seeking total uniformity of opinion, and neither should the author. Each reviewer's feedback will give something new to ponder. Only when they are completely opposed would the editor seek a third opinion or override with his or her own judgement.

That quality of exclusivity, the 'old-boy network', has long been a weakness of the review process and people are right to criticize it. Unfortunately, no one has yet devised a better alternative. The only advice has to be: if you can't beat them, join them. Subjecting your paper to review by close and trusted colleagues first is, as we will discuss later, a good way to prepare yourself for the review board itself.

What do authors do to make the review process more difficult?

Poor targeting

Unlike most editors, reviewers will read each paper closely with pen in hand to make notes. The editor's job has been to put the paper into the review process if it generally seems to suit the journal's objectives; the reviewer puts the detailed time into reading it. So, why infuriate them by not paying attention to the journal's nature?

One reviewer who saw that a paper did not properly reflect the aims of the journal was moved to write:

The Notes for Contributors states 'The objective of the journal is to provide practitioners with new ideas that will be applicable to their daily work. Each article must put forth recommendations as to how the material contained in the article can be utilised in business practice'. This paper offers no recommendations to business people ... I really see no way this paper would be of interest to practitioners.

Back to the word processor!

Poor proofreading

There are no excuses for spelling or punctuation mistakes. Not only would this confuse your reader, but it slows the reviewer down and causes immense frustration that someone appears to have such little respect for the subject matter or the readership. Remember that the reviewer is trying to make a fair judgement about the paper and offer constructive feedback. Don't put obstacles in his or her way.

You can help the reviewer do his or her job more easily by:

Detailed adherence to the Notes for Authors

This aspect is covered in detail in Chapter 9. It not only helps your paper get into the review stream, but it ensures that an overworked reviewer won't dismiss it lightly. At least it will be read.

Checking your work

Use your computer spell-check, but remember it won't recognize all mistakes, such as their/there, our/hour/are, its/it's. Ask a colleague or friend to read it. Again, we'll discuss techniques later on.

There's much more to do to make a paper acceptable but, at the very least, the points above will allay your reviewers' obvious concerns.

Summary

Authors need to recognize their position in a larger chain. By putting ourselves in the position of others in the chain we are more likely to see how the publishing process benefits everyone. Of most immediate interest to the author are the editor, reviewer and reader. The needs of the publisher and those involved in checking the manuscript are discussed later.

Writing may sometimes seem a lonely job, but next time you are sweating over a paper at midnight, consider the overworked editor and reviewer who is doing much the same.

Action points

Here's an interesting exercise. Keep any direct mail that arrives at your home or office over the next week or so. When you have collected a small pile, sit down for an hour and pick out the two best communications and two worst. What makes the good ones good, and the bad ones bad? You will probably find that the good ones are good because they have, by accident or planning, somehow touched some need or desire or personal chord, and the bad ones are bad because they have studiously paid no attention whatsoever to who you are.

No, you aren't being schooled as a direct mail campaign planner. But this exercise will help you pick up some tips on how to structure an unsolicited communication so that it has more chance of hitting the spot with the editor, and his or her teams. And that's a useful skill.

8 Through the reader's eyes

Have you ever looked at your holiday photos and cursed yourself for not capturing a moment as you recall it? The people sitting around the poolside never look quite as you remember them; the sunset doesn't appear quite as red and purple as it was, and where is the hotel garden that you remember so vividly? Unless you happen to be a professional photographer, you will probably find that your photos rarely reflect all that you saw at the time. That's because what you saw through the lens bore little resemblance to what you really saw. The wider landscape taken in by your peripheral vision, the voices of the people in the photograph and how you felt at the time was part of the whole.

When we write an article we are, in essence, taking a snapshot of what we know at the time. We, of course, remember all the background to the paper and many of the reasons why we did what we did. In other words, our peripheral vision is still compensating for us. As we have seen in earlier chapters, perspectives of the world differ depending upon who is looking at it. In our own egocentric universe we see our paper in its complete form and understand not only what appears on the pages but what went into its making. The reader, however, has no peripheral vision, and we will not be sitting beside him or her narrating the piece as we might when we show a friend our holiday pictures. For the readers, what they see is what they get.

A common complaint of reviewers is that the author did not view the paper through the reader's eyes. This caused one reviewer to comment:

> A substantial amount of work is required before publication can be entertained. The author would do well to attempt to approach his/her material from the readers' perspective.

This perspective is learned, rather than inherent. We have to make an effort to see the world through our readers' eyes, as our natural inclination is to see it through our own.

In this chapter we will analyse more closely who our readers are and find ways to put ourselves in their place. We need to ask, who are the people reading the journal? Do you ever read the journal? If you do, then you are halfway there: those who will read your paper are people like you. They are keen to learn, eager to share and hope to stay up to date. You know they must be if they are reading the journal in the first place.

Because an academic journal is by nature highly specialized, you can be sure that few people are picking it up for an idle browse. Anyone who begins to read it is interested and involved in the subject area. While that narrows the list of potential readers, it does raise uncertainties about the reader's own level of expertise in the subject. The reader may be a student, approaching the subject for the first time, or a renowned expert. What benefits do they seek in common? How do we enter their minds?

Knowing what readers want

A brutal fact about publishing any kind of article is that the readers are not interested in the article at all. No matter how long it took us to craft, no matter how many years of work went into the research, the reader doesn't care in the least. Indeed, many readers of the journal will not read our article word-for-word, but, rather, will skip through it for the key points. Only if that results in them being even more interested will they bother to go back through it line-by-line. The earlier we capture readers' interest, the more likely they are to read the whole article.

> This paper describes work which is under way to develop sound qualitative methods for risk assessment. A specific focus of this work is the development of a computer-based assistant for the assessment of the potential carcinogenic risk of chemical compounds. However, the approach should have much wider application. (Krause and Fox, 1994)

The authors who began their paper thus knew what was interesting about their research and were determined to tell readers about it immediately.

While we may not be able to meet readers personally, we will be able to make certain assumptions about them merely because they read that particular journal. We can assume, for example, that if the journal specializes in fast-breaking research news rather than in-depth conceptual discourses that our reader is trying to stay in the forefront of current empirical research. Coming to those conclusions is the basis of our next chapter on targeting journals. For now, at least we know that we can segment the great world of potential readers into at least a fairly narrow band of readers attracted to a particular journal. We now know that they are interested in the same sort of papers that we are, or they wouldn't be reading the journal and we wouldn't be writing for it.

And yet, as we know ourselves because of how we read journals, many readers will never read the article at all but will only read the abstract. Some may pick up the journal to read the abstract while others will glance at it on an electronic database. If someone were to invent a quick, foolproof way to assimilate all the relevant information from a paper without actually having to sit down and work through it, people would gladly give up reading papers.

What the reader wants is not the words themselves but the information within them. The previous discussions on product- versus market-orientation should leave that as no surprise. It is not the product (article) that is important but the benefits it confers.

Readers, like all consumers, have certain expectations of the product that they consume. They are not confused about what they expect. When my organization conducted its quality study, described in Chapter 6, we found consistent agreement amongst readers, authors, editors and reviewers. Those who were familiar with the journal were almost united in how they rated it. Had we found large sections of discrepancy we would have concluded that the journal was not well positioned and that it had a market that was unsure about what it wanted. Instead, we found that the way people viewed each journal was unique per journal, but common within its readership.

Writing a paper for any given journal therefore involves the author in an undertaking to the reader. If the reader is expecting descriptions of innovative research applied in practice, then that is what we must deliver. If the reader is expecting a quick overview of where leading-edge research is heading, with implications for other researchers, then that is what the author must provide. We can't set up expectations only to disappoint, as happened to the reviewer who wrote:

> I started reading this paper with great interest. Unfortunately, I was disappointed. The article reads more like a textbook.

Readers, like any kind of consumer, think worse of people who raised their hopes only to dash them than they do of those who promised less but delivered more.

The only question left for the author is: how do we help the reader approach and continue with our article?

The five-minute test

In 1995 I introduced a discipline for my colleagues and students to use when assessing the quality of articles. The objective was to be able to judge quickly whether an article met any reader's basic requirements. If it did not even meet basic standards then it would not qualify as an article deserving a specialist's attention. This simple exercise helps us assess the baseline quality of any article whatever the subject and whatever the background of a reader.

Our assumption is that readers are busy people – people like us – who must navigate through a large pool of information for the ideas or evidence they need. We also assume that if they cannot judge whether a paper will deliver the benefits required, they will seek another article that will. The foundation for our assumptions lies not only in common sense, but in what editors, authors and reviewers have said. Using the exercise in practice with people from fields as diverse as education, science, management and the humanities, we have discovered what every researcher longs for – and it works every time.

An author's professionalism is the ability to judge his or her work objectively. Given how difficult we all find being objective about ourselves, the exercise can be used not only to help you assess your own work but to fine-tune your sensitivity to what is, or is not, a good article.

We have discussed in previous chapters the importance reviewers attach to the purpose and implications of an article. We also know from what they tell us and our own experience that any communication should be clear and its message comprehensible, even if it is unusual or technical. The qualities of readability will be discussed in much more detail in Chapter 12. Doing the exercise now will help you see how easy it is to decide whether or not an article is worth reading.

Pick up, at random, any journal in any subject area. Choose an article, again at random, about anything at all. You will be assessing the article using five criteria:

1   **Purpose**: clearly stated on the first page?
2   **Key points**: logically flowing from point to point with signposting, such as subheadings, introductions and conclusions to sections?
3   **Implications**: clearly specified, with special attention to who the implications are for and what readers can do next?
4   **Readability**: jargon-free, familiar words, reasonably short sentences, easy to follow theme?
5   **Appeal**: Would you like to go back and read the article more thoroughly?

Allow yourself precisely five minutes for the exercise. Scan the article and, under each heading, make a couple of notes. At the end of the five minutes review your piece of paper. Do your own notes tell you, without any doubt, what the article is about, what are its main points and what are its implications? Could you understand what the author was saying even if you did not understand the nuances of the subject area? Most importantly, would you go back and read it thoroughly?

This exercise has been used to give an initial evaluation of literally thousands of articles, and it has never been proved wrong. Any article that has not met these five criteria in five minutes is a poor-quality article. Whatever the originality or usefulness of its message, if a quick scan cannot bring those points home immediately to the reader, the article fails. Why does it fail? Because it is less likely to be read by a reader, who seeks information now not in a few months' time when he or she has worked up the energy to tackle it again.

By doing this exercise the reader will not understand the author's subject in detail; indeed, it may take hours and several rereadings for the reader to absorb all the meaning. It may take days or weeks before the reader has truly come to grips with the enormity and complexity of the research and begins to use it. But the exercise only models what we readers – you, they and I – do all the time. We scan, we browse, we sift. As a brief aside, I often find it surprising how many people doing this exercise comment: 'It's not my field, but the author made it sound so interesting that I would definitely read it again.' Unfortunately, those comments are too often balanced against the ones that read: 'No idea what this person is droning on about or why. I would dread having to read it in depth.'

Readers want access to the right information they can understand and use. Given a choice between a turgid, vague paper and a paper which, on a quick scan, reveals what you are looking for, which one would you choose? In Chapters 10, 11 and 12 we will work through in detail exactly how to structure and write articles that will pass the five-minute test with honours.

Hidden questions

As they open a journal readers are rapidly running through a series of questions. Part of understanding the reader is to understand those questions. Remember, they're the same questions that we all ask.

While writing, and again once your draft is complete, ask yourself:

- Will my reader want to know this? Why?
- Will my reader understand? Why?
- Will my reader care? Why?

Your reader has many of the same questions in mind as has your editor and reviewer.

Is it interesting?

This is the 'discovery' factor that must be present in a good academic paper. The reader must experience a moment of truth, feel a frisson of excitement, glimpse a new picture. Otherwise, your article is merely reiterating what everyone else already knows and will probably, for this reason alone, never get past the review board. Many referees comment that although papers are well written and describe sound research, they just aren't interesting.

> Neither the underlying propositions nor the research method offer interest. The topic is of great importance; however, this is not the way to go about it.

Perhaps the author who inspired the above reviewer's comment had lost interest too. Maybe, halfway through the research he or she rushed it through and quickly wrote it to meet a neglected deadline. Or, maybe the author simply lost sight of what was interesting in the first place.

Make sure that you understand what your new angle is. You may be so familiar with it that it seems ordinary by now. You may have forgotten your own excitement when you experienced the moment of insight. Perhaps you have now moved on to new research and this writing-up of last year's findings is becoming tedious. Before you go any further, apply the 20-words-or less rule: what is it that will strike your reader's attention? What is it that is interesting about your paper? Once you know, you'll be able to communicate it to your reader.

But how can you be sure it's not just you who thinks it's interesting? How will you know if it is interesting to your reader? The only way to find out what people want or think is to ask them. It's that simple, and that difficult. Many authors, particularly new ones, are nervous about exposing their work to others. We've been through many of their reasons for this in the initial chapters of this book, but it's worth reminding ourselves now that it is often this fear that prevents people from asking for constructive criticism.

As an exercise, do your 20-words-or-less exercise and then talk to a colleague informally. Ask him or her to listen to you briefly describe why you think your work is interesting. Accept their feedback and consider whether you need to change the angle. Finally, make sure you aren't just playing with words. The interest you spark at the beginning must be maintained.

Can I understand it?

Even people new to the discipline must be able to make sense of your paper. We will discuss in Chapter 12 essential points of style, but for now we must concentrate on empathy with the reader. Just because you have been close to your research for five years doesn't mean that someone new to your ideas will be able to grasp them quickly.

There's a fine line between patronizing the reader and being arrogant about your knowledge. You can find that balance by recognizing the difference between form and content: your new material may be surprising to your readers, but they shouldn't have any difficulty comprehending what you are saying. Understand the assumptions you are making. Go through a silent dialogue with your reader as you write. Do you really expect, for example, all your readers to be completely familiar with the literature that underpins your research? The most common purpose of a literature review is to give the reader the relevant background that enables him or her to understand the author's research in context. One reviewer described it this way:

> The paper needs to start with a better review of the literature. Go into more detail with previous research and try to relate the results to previous findings.

Are you confident that readers know what techniques you are describing? You may have used an advanced technique that may be unfamiliar to many of your readers and requires further explanation. Or you may be using a common tool but have not explained why you chose it or how you used it. Never assume too much; otherwise, be prepared for reviewer's comments such as these below:

> More justification is needed as to how the questionnaire was developed. What was the justification for including some of the questions? Also, for many of the questions it is unclear how they were measured (i.e. what scales). It may be helpful to have the questionnaire included in an appendix.

Can I use it?

We explored fully the importance of implications in Chapter 4. Here, we should note the links between the implications and the reader. Each readership may have a slightly different way of applying the findings or furthering the research. This needs to be fully detailed; never end your articles with the words 'more research is needed'. By whom? Looking into what?

> We observed that the fuzzy MLP was translation invariant in classifying the fingerprint patterns with respect to the input window. We plan to extend the model in future to be rotation variant as well. (Mitra and Kundu, 1994)

Although I must admit that I don't know my translation invariants from my rotations, I have no doubt that a regular reader of *Neural Computing and Applications* would be confident about the authors' implications.

Summary

This chapter has dealt with understanding the needs of readers. We can assume they are people just like us but that, unlike us, they have no interest in our paper *per se*, only in the information we give them. Whether it takes us 1000 words or 12 000 to explain the message, our readers will stay with us if we make it obvious what the benefits are for them.

Authors need to face the uncomfortable truth that, unless a reader is forced to read a paper, he or she will always choose one which meets their expectations quickly, clearly and easily. We all have better things to do with our time than subject ourselves to unnecessary work, and readers now have more choices than ever before. Apart from the helpful side-benefit of curing insomnia, we will not read papers that leave us bored and confused with any enthusiasm – if we read them at all.

Fortunately, it will not take too much effort to learn how to write papers which gain and maintain your reader's interest. In the next chapter, we will find ways to match our interest with a journal's interest and eventually satisfy, perhaps even delight, its readers.

Action points

Note, in 20 words or less, what is it that will seize your reader's attention? What is it that is interesting about your paper? Once you know, you'll be able to communicate it to your reader.

Now try the five-minute test. Pick up, at random, any journal in any subject area. Choose an article, again at random, about anything at all. Look for:

- **Purpose**: clearly stated on the first page?
- **Key points**: logically flowing from point to point with signposting, such as subheadings, introductions and conclusions to sections?
- **Implications**: clearly specified, with special attention to who the implications are for and what they can do next?
- **Readability**: jargon-free, familiar words, reasonably short sentences, easy to follow theme?
- **Appeal**: would you like to go back and read the article more thoroughly?

Note all these points, and do the exercise in five minutes or less. Make a habit of regularly making a five-minute scan of articles. You will quickly see which authors can survive a scan and encourage their readers to think 'Yes, I'd really like to give this some serious thought', and which seem to pay scant attention to the communication process. Once you understand this, you can apply the technique to your own work.

9 Targeting journals

Most editors say that many of the manuscripts they receive don't even reach the review stage. They are immediately rejected because they do not meet the editorial objectives of the journal.

> When we receive a manuscript, we decide whether to send it for peer review on the basis of its suitability for *Nature* (novel, of broad general interest, arresting, a clear conceptual advance, free of obvious flaws, well written). Of the manuscripts, between half and a quarter are sent for review. (Dr Maxine Clark, Executive Editor, *Nature*)

This chapter is about how to target journals, how to learn what editors want and how to make sure you are providing a manuscript to fit their requirements. The objective at this stage is to have the article reviewed. In the first three chapters of Part III we will discuss in detail how to structure and style articles to meet various quality criteria. For the moment, we need to know that those who matter will read the article.

Who are you writing for?

The academic publishing industry is tough and precise. Journals are a product, like soft drinks and soap powder, created for a group of people with recognized needs. They are packaged, sold and delivered. Strong publishers survive; the weak fail.

Like any new product, launching a journal is a highly risky business. This is true both for commercial publishers and learned societies or institutions who have a house journal. The only difference is that the commercial publisher is totally reliant on income from its journals whereas the society or institution can often cross-subsidize from other sources of income – although only to a point. The commercial publisher sets the subscription price at, say, £100. The society says the membership fee is £100, which includes a journal and often little else. In either case, the financial performance of the journal is important. It must sell subscriptions.

Subscriptions to scholarly journals are sold largely to librarians. The librarian may take advice from others, such as departments' library committees or from other library users, but will make a final choice based on the budget available. A librarian's budget covers not only journal subscriptions, but books and administration. A key criterion for the librarian's decision is: is the journal value for money? The only way to determine this is to find out whether the journal is being read, but this is a notoriously difficult task. Some librarians monitor usage through surveys; some regularly examine the journals on their shelves to see if the pages have been thumbed through.

Few journals in the academic field are bought in large numbers. Many focus so tightly on a particular niche that they will only be of interest to a few thousand, or even a few hundred, institutions. What is important is not how many sell, as a price can be established for a low-volume journal that still justifies its expense, but how it is selling against the forecast and, most importantly, against the forecasted renewals.

Whether or not people renew their subscriptions depends on whether they are satisfied with the journal. That means the journal must continue to appeal to its target audience. The appeal will come, as we discussed in the previous chapter not from the cover design or even the respected names on the advisory board, but from the content. If the content does not reflect the interests of the audience, the audience will go elsewhere.

To be clear about the audience's interests, publishers and editors work closely together to establish the journal's editorial objectives, explore the kinds of papers likely to meet those objectives and create clear guidelines for potential authors. Editors brief members of the review board thoroughly on the journal's objectives. Indeed, many of the pro-formas set by journals for the reviewers ask the direct question: 'Does the paper reflect the editorial objectives of the journal?'

Why, then, are up to half of all papers rejected before the review process? And, why do some of those which are reviewed engender comments such as those below, given by a reviewer of a well-focused, highly academic journal:

> The topic itself is interesting but the treatment from an academic standpoint is slightly shallow. ... This is the kind of paper which is probably more of interest to practitioners than to academics.

Perhaps the author didn't bother to investigate the journal's objectives, or perhaps the paper was rejected by the author's preferred journal and simply sent on to the next without revision. Or maybe the author just didn't know how to research the targeted journal. Whatever the reason, you have no excuse now. What follows is a detailed guide on how to find the right journal and, most importantly, how to find out exactly what sort of paper the journal requires.

Let us assume first that you are starting from a position of relative ignorance. You've worked out the purpose and implication of your paper, you understand who your readers are, but now you have to find them. There are several sources of information that are set out below in what is probably the best chronological sequence for authors to adopt.

First sources of information

Directories

If you have no idea about any of the prospective journals that might suit your paper, you can always refer to a directory of publications. Your librarian will have at least one directory in the library. While the directory's information can be helpful, particularly for gaining a quick overview of the journal, it will only give you a superficial feel for what the journal requires. Directories are inevitably out of date. Even last year's directory won't tell you the name of a recently appointed new editor.

Respected authors

You will be familiar with the leaders in your own field and will know who is writing about topics closely linked to yours. You can find out where these authors are published by carrying out a search by author in your library. You can also find out where those who cite them are being published by referring to a citation index. But, again, this only gives you a list of prospective journals. It doesn't give you any in-depth information about the journals or their editors.

Respected colleagues and authorities

Find out which journals matter most to those in a position to judge you. Which journals are rated most highly by members of your appointments committees? Which journals do government assessment teams use for their purposes? Which do your professors, bosses and supervisors read? These are the people you need to impress for promotion or funding; some may even be journal reviewers. The unavoidable rule about being judged by other people is to always find out what criteria they are using. If your reference group rates one journal more highly than another, you need to know – and why.

Ask around. What do the people you most respect read? What do they have to say about the journals you have shortlisted? Where do they publish, and where did they publish first? What alternatives do they know to the journals you have selected? Is there a slightly different angle you could take to gain acceptance by a journal that may be more narrowly focused, but no less respected?

Going deeper

At best, your research so far will only give you a brief overview of the journals that might be suitable and the names and addresses of editors. Unfortunately, this is where too many authors stop. It's a little like going to a dating agency and simply finding out your date's first name and telephone number. What are you going to talk about over dinner? Before you write your paper, you will need a thorough idea of the journal's requirements. Finding these out is easy but takes time.

Reading journals

To understand a journal you must learn to read it critically, looking beyond the obvious for hints below the surface. Copies may be available in your own library, or the librarian may be able to obtain them through interlibrary loans. You may be tempted to pick up any copy lying around, or ask the librarian for the last two or three issues. Without doubt you should read several issues – three is probably a minimum. After all, your objective is to become familiar with the journal, not just to know how to spell its name. But, which three should you choose?

The first and last issues in any one volume (year) are those which will probably contain the most clues since it is in these issues that strategically-minded editors discuss their objectives. In the first issue editors, who will usually have several months' or even a year's copy held in advance, will often describe what themes are to come. As they anticipate the new year, they will also often comment on the kinds of papers they hope to receive, or the improvements they will be making to the journal. In the last issue, editors will often summarize the year's contributions and comment on what they consider to be the high and low points.

Most publishers will respond to a direct written request for a sample copy of the journal. Having your own copy is convenient and allows you to make notes against published articles. You should do this in addition to reading several issues thoroughly.

Notes to Authors

All journals publish Notes for prospective authors. Most carry them in each issue but if they do not there will be a reference to them and to the issue in which they appear. The Notes vary in detail from general to specific. At the very least, and of most importance to the author, they should include the editorial objectives. The examples below illustrate how clearly some top-class journals state their objectives:

> *Psychological Review* publishes articles that make important theoretical contributions to any area of scientific psychology. Preference is given to papers that advance theory rather than review it and to statements that are specifically theoretical rather than programmatic. Papers that point up critical flaws in existing theory or demonstrate the superiority of one theory over another will also be considered. Papers devoted primarily to surveys of literature, problems of method and design, or reports of empirical findings are ordinarily not appropriate. Discussions of previously published articles will be considered for publication as Theoretical Notes on the basis of the scientific contribution represented.

> The *World Economy* concentrates on trade policy issues both on a country basis, regionally (EC, ASEAN, North America, Asia-Pacific, etc.) and globally (GATT and other fora). The *World Economy* does, however, also cover broader issues (exchange rates, IMF/World Bank, debt, environmental or other international issues) as they relate to trade.

> The editors welcome manuscripts written for a broad audience of professional biologists and for advanced students. *BioScience* publishes peer-reviewed articles, summarising recent advances in important areas of biological research.

The Notes for *BioScience* continue by describing the other sections of the journal where contributions are welcomed, and then gives further guidance on what is being sought from articles:

> Articles should review significant scientific findings in an area of interest to a broad range of biologists. They should include background for biologists in disparate fields. The writing should be free of jargon. All articles, whether invited or independently submitted, undergo peer review of content and writing style. Articles must be no longer than 20–25 double-spaced typed pages, including all figures, tables and references. No more than 50 references should be cited.

The above examples are good illustrations of clear and pointed Notes to Authors. There leave no doubt as to the direction of the journals described, and therefore leave the contributor no excuse for submitting anything less than appropriate, nor any reason why the editor or reviewers should tolerate anything less.

The Notes in most journals continue beyond editorial objectives to specify how authors should present papers. This is known in the industry as the journal's house style. It's a sure give-away that authors have not researched the journal when they submit papers in a completely different format than that required. We'll discuss presentation in more detail in

Part III, but the objectives here are to make sure that you target the right journal and begin to plan the article in accordance with that journal's objectives.

The editor's perspective

Read the editorials. What does the editor say about the current issue of the journal? Note comments like 'Brown's paper on the use of slang in Puerto Rico is a good example of the literature springing to life as it is tested in practice'. That's a fairly clear statement of what the editor likes to see in a paper. Other editorials might centre on topical issues that capture the editor's attention; conversely, some may indicate topics or treatments of topics that the editor finds overworked. A month after an editor has sworn never to publish yet another treatise on the wheel of retailing is not the time to send him your brilliant summary of it. Again, editorial preference is likely to be more clearly stated in the first and last issues of a volume.

Editors will often comment on a paper that has made a particular impact, and discuss the reasons why. Each of the journals published by MCB University Press has an annual Best Paper Award, the results of which are published in the individual journals. John Wiley & Sons runs similar initiatives for its *Strategic Management Journal*. Perhaps consistent with a journal of that title, the annual 'best' paper is always one judged to have had an impact since its publication which must have been more than five years earlier. Many other journals have equally important awards.

When the editorial direction of a journal changes, this too will be commented on in an editorial. A change in direction often accompanies a change in editor. Discussion of the new editor's ambitions will offer further insight into the future of the journal and the papers being sought. The following example shows how revealing these points can be.

'Effective January 1 1995, Robert Feenestra has taken over from Richard Brecher as Editor of the *Journal of International Economics*,' began an announcement in the first pages of the journal. After thanking the previous editor for his contribution, the announcement continued by reporting on several forthcoming changes:

> ... decentralising editorial decisions to the Co-Editors; publishing at least one symposium or an issue of topical interest annually; encouraging publication of applied and macroeconomic financial papers (See the revised Aims and Scope on the inside cover of this issue) ... .

Not only will observing editors' comments help you judge how best to approach your paper, but referring to them in any correspondence will impress the editor that you are taking your job seriously and, at the very least, improve the chances of starting discussions. Submitting a written synopsis of your paper accompanied by a letter which begins 'Your observation in Vol. 12 No. 6 that little work has been done to research the effects of carbon monoxide on pond flora helped me direct the paper that I am now preparing' is quite impressive.

Reading the editor's own articles will give you further information about his or her background and needs. Many editors are well published; finding their articles will not be difficult. What does he or she say about the field in which you are both working? What work has the editor done which impacts on your own? The objective here is not to be sycophantic: you're not searching for a clone of an editor nor are you seeking to fall into the trap of becoming afraid to challenge existing theory particularly when that theory may be the editor's. Good editors warm to a fair challenge.

What is important is the knowledge base upon which you are building. The information that your targeted editor has written 17 articles about the very subject you have been researching will help you tailor your covering letter. Don't think for a moment that an editor will be unmoved by a letter that starts: 'Although I agreed with you in Vol. 6 No. 2 that the Canadian presence during the fall of Hong Kong has been under-researched, I think after reading the enclosed manuscript you may agree that there are less than obvious reasons why this is so'.

Reviewers' perspectives

Although in a blind review process the reviewer supposedly doesn't know the author and vice versa, we have to remember that it's a small world. Particularly if you write about a highly specialized topic, it is likely that only a handful of people would be competent enough to comment on it. From scanning the review board, usually published in at least one issue of each volume, it should be easy to pick out the few most likely to read your submission.

Who are they? Do you know what they have written? Do you know their particular sensitivities? Find out! Just by reading their own articles you may begin to understand their own quality criteria. Maybe the professor has written in a recent paper that the early work of Dr So-and-so has received scant attention, and you just happen to agree. Perhaps you can say so a little more clearly in your manuscript. Once again, the objective here is not to change your purpose, findings or implications. No one will build a credible career writing papers simply to mirror a reviewer's viewpoint, and the risk of your paper being sent to another reviewer who fundamentally disagrees is probably too great. But if the reviewers are consistently asking for certain points and you can do it, then do it. If they are noted for their own characteristically jargon-free papers, purge your own.

Quality criteria

Write to the editor and ask for a statement of quality criteria. This should go well beyond the guidance notes given in the journal. You need to know how editors and reviewers make their decisions. What exactly do they look for? Many journals have a pro forma which guides their reviewers. Write to the editor of your chosen journal and ask for one.

As we found with our own benchmarking exercises, people who read and influence the journal are very clear about the criteria. The results, when we asked people to rank and weight journals, were consistent per journal. It was not difficult to analyse the results and get a clear profile. This means that readers, editors and reviewers of well focused journals know what the journal stands for. It is only one step further to ask the readers, editors and reviewers to articulate their understanding and convert the results into practical guidelines for authors. As this becomes easier, with good data management, it will increasingly become the norm.

As a prospective author for a selected journal, you not only have the right but even the responsibility to demand clear statements of quality criteria from the editor and publisher. A journal that cannot articulate this, and is unwilling to share it, is a journal with a questionable future.

Clues from articles

The published papers themselves will give you further insight. Make a habit of deconstructing them against quality criteria. Use the five-minute test detailed in the previous chapter to assess baseline quality.

Authors who consistently contribute to the same journals will frequently refer to articles previously published in the journal. You can do an online search restricting the areas to keyword for subject and journal. This will give you a list of articles published in your area in the journals you are targeting. You can then create a map showing how the journal has traced the development of your topic, and what previously published authors have said and how.

Building on the body of knowledge therefore becomes a more careful exercise, given that your targeted journals are those you have decided are the best places to publish your material. Working from that assumption, it is only reasonable to cite their contributions to the body of knowledge.

Widening the field

Suppose you are not starting from scratch? What if you are absolutely convinced that there is only one journal worth writing for? Think again. Ask yourself why you are concentrating exclusively on one outlet. There may be other good journals that may not be as widely known as your selected journal, but which are respected within their area.

One of the more serious pitfalls awaiting authors is their conviction that they know a journal well simply because they have heard a great deal about it, or have seen it referenced frequently. That journal may therefore be popular, and for many good reasons, but it is not necessarily the only one available. It is still wise to go through the exercises described above, even if you believe you will commit yourself to one journal. Test your up-to-date knowledge about the journal by reading it and contacting the editor and publisher as discussed above. Don't allow yourself to be blinkered by your own convictions, particularly if you have little empiri-cal proof for your conclusions.

During the course of our benchmarking study we asked authors to name the chief competitors of the journals we were researching. That question generated between three and 12 responses, with an average of four competitors per journal. These were journals that, in the authors' opinions, were alternative sources of publication. As an exercise, list as many complementary journals as you can for the journal you are now targeting. If you find this exercise difficult, it may be time to check the directories and get to know the full range of journals available to you.

Trying it on

Now that you have a shortlist of potential journals and are well acquainted with what they publish and how, you may decide to approach the editor with your idea. Many journals actively encourage this for specific sec-tions:

Section Editors will be happy to discuss drafts and proposed contributions with contributors.

News and Views articles inform nonspecialist readers about new scientific ad-vances, sometimes in the form of a conference report. Most are commissioned but proposals can be made in advance to the News and Views Editor.

But what about synopses of your full article? Editors' propensities to welcome initial enquiries vary from journal to journal. Some expect au-thors to be familiar with the journal and its requirements, making the synopsis stage not only unnecessary but tedious. Their view is if the author knows what to do and how to do it, why doesn't he or she just get on with it? Why waste the editor's time in the interim, reading a lengthy and sometimes boring synopsis? These editors only make their judge-ments on the finished article. There are, however, other editors who ap-preciate an author first testing the idea. This would be more likely in a fast-moving field where the journal rapidly turns articles into print before they go out of date. An editor of that kind of journal may already have an article or two poised for publication that covers exactly the same material you may have in mind. If you do decide to write a synopsis first, make sure you do it properly. It would be a shame for your potentially good article never to get into print merely because you described it poorly in a synopsis. More guidance is given in Chapter 10.

Summary

We have explored in this chapter how important it is to target the correct journal. By now, you have now done the hardest part of the work: re-searching your audience, targeting your journals, understanding what they expect and planning how to meet those expectations. The next chapter will help you bring it all together.

Action points

Now it's time to start some research. Select from your library, or by some other means, between two and four 'target' journals for your article. Go through the Notes for Authors and make notes. What is the scope? What is the preferred length? How many copies should you send? Normally, a reviewed journal will ask for three copies minimum; one for the editor to hold on file and two for the reviewers. Few things annoy an editor more than having to request extra copies, or wait in the queue for the photo-copier to reproduce what an author couldn't be bothered to do. What's the referencing style? Are there any peculiarities such as 'Every paper should conclude with a list of "Points to note" for practitioners'?

Next, examine the journal's contents. Read some articles. Read the editorials. Note the names on the advisory board and review board, if listed. Is anyone there whose work you know?

Now you have a relationship in preparation. All you have to do is deliver the goods … .

PART III

From draft to print

10 Seven days to a finished paper

Writing an academic paper in a week? This is what this book is all about – finishing a paper as quickly and effortlessly as possible. And, the good news is that it is possible to do it in less than a week. Writing is the easy part. Having done the hard preparatory work, you can write a good academic paper in a couple of days. But first, you need to consider the specific questions posed in the previous chapters. Next, you need to create a plan for the article. Then, you need to create a detailed outline. Finally – and here's the enjoyable part – you can write it.

Not every paper is worth writing. Some are not yet ready because either the research is incomplete or your thoughts about the implications are not well developed. Others are ready to be written but there does not seem to be a suitable journal that is rated highly enough amongst one's reference group. Like any activity, there will be competing time or resource pressures that force you to set priorities.

This chapter describes how to prioritize potential papers to help you plan the work ahead and select the right paper for immediate attention.

Towards a strategy

When new authors worry about where to start they are usually considering much more than what words to use first. They want to know what kind of article to write as a result of their research and what kind of journal might publish it. Frequently, they fail to recognize the numerous possibilities that exist for a single piece of research they can write about in different ways for different audiences.

The great strategic thinker Igor Ansoff (Ansoff, 1965) provided organizations with a model to help them plan what to do with their products and potential markets. He suggested that there are four variables that offer different opportunities when differently combined: new products, existing products, new markets, existing markets. Translating this concept to papers and journals we might look at it this way: unwritten papers, written papers, unfamiliar journals, familiar journals. What choices does this give us?

Unwritten papers to unfamiliar journals

This is the riskiest option. We have not yet tested our ideas by writing them down and we know nothing about the journal we are targeting. Our minds must be full of uncertainty and doubt: how do we write it, where do we start, how do we know if it is suitable for the journal? Having already noted the importance of understanding clearly the nature of our purpose and implications, and having realized the importance of understanding the editorial board's and readers' perspectives, we know this option is the least attractive. Unfortunately, that's where many new writers start – and stop. Let's reject this as a viable option, unless we decide to make it our business to find out enough about the journal to make it familiar.

Unwritten papers to familiar journals

Now we are heading in the right direction. We have not yet written the paper, yet we have thought through what's important about it and familiarized ourselves with the appropriate journal. We can plan now in more detail with the needs of the journal and its interested parties to guide us.

Written papers to unfamiliar journals

The paper has been written, or even published, and we may be happy with it but are now increasing our risk of rejection by sending it to a journal we don't know. Even if the paper has appeared elsewhere first, many journals will consider an adaptation of the original to suit their own readership. The original, for example, might have been a lengthy research-based paper of interest to other researchers, but another journal directed at practitioners may welcome a shorter, more practically-oriented piece for its readers. Our problem will be understanding how to adapt it if we have not yet made ourselves aware of the journal's needs.

It is a good idea to widen the field as much as possible. Too many authors restrict themselves to the one or two journals they know, without finding out about related journals. Sending a paper to a top-rated journal with a rejection rate of 98 per cent is a rather discouraging way to start. Of course, everyone in their respective fields lusts after the *Harvard Business Review*, *The Lancet*, or *Nature*, but few are chosen. Better to practise on a journal that has several hundred, rather than several thousand, papers from which to choose.

Written papers to familiar journals

Now that we have a paper that meets our own quality criteria, it's a small step to adapt it to the criteria of a journal we know. This sometimes happens when authors rework a published paper to a new angle for a different journal. Creative authors can derive several papers from the original in this way. Say, for example, the first paper was a 10 000-word detailed description of the research just completed. The objective was to report the findings for the first time, and therefore the author selected a journal positioned as a publication of original, new research findings. (Some journals will accept nothing less than being the first to report the news.) Having published in that journal, the author takes the 10 000 words, cuts it to 5000 by removing much of the method section, modifies the literature review to give a broad, general background to the subject and sends it to a journal interested in how research can be applied in practice. The same author can boil the whole paper down to 1000 words and send it to a popular magazine and newspaper, which, if nothing else, is the best possible exercise to tone up clarity and style.

Strategic options are therefore available to make the author's job more manageable and also give a longer-term approach to the other papers not yet ready for writing.

Your plan

Let's start with a review of where we have reached so far. By now you may have worked through the ideas contained in the earlier chapters and are ready to work on the article itself. Take a few moments now to summarize progress.

This is also the time to force yourself to appraise your work through the readers' eyes. Step back and evaluate what the reader needs to know. If you don't, you will find your reader is unable to share with you the excitement and value of your work. Once confusion sets in, there is no communication, just a one-way monologue, as one reviewer noted:

> Although the English is good, I found it difficult to follow. The authors are too close to the topic to be able to describe in terms easily understandable to those not familiar with the techniques.

Writing a synopsis of the paper is a good place to start, whether or not it becomes appropriate to send it to an editor. A synopsis will help clarify your own thoughts by forcing you to articulate the key points. Before you start you need to know where the article will be placed. This will ensure that you structure, angle and write it suitably for your audience. By the time you finish this section you will be completely familiar with the journal and its editorial board: you will have no lingering doubts about who these people are and what they want. You will also be clear about how your article will meet the journal's objectives because you will create a statement under each heading declaring exactly how you will be complying with the objectives.

To prepare for this, make notes against the headings we have already discussed. Try to keep the notes to only a sentence or two – 20 words or less is ideal. Make sure that your thoughts are clear about headings 1 and 2 before proceeding to the next

1   **Purpose**
2   **Implications**
3   **Target audience** (journal, readership)

- editorial objectives:

    - take these from the Notes for Authors
    - add new points you have found from reading the editorials.

- editorial pen-sketch:

    - a short description of the main editor: position, length of service, own articles
    - a short description of relevant section editors
    - main reviewers likely to read your manuscript and any clues you have about them.

- style (length and tone):

    - take from Notes for Authors
    - add new points from editorials, reviewers' checklist and from reading the journal.

- target readership:

    - take from the Notes for Authors
    - add new points from editorials and reviewer's checklist or pro forma.

4   **Benefits being sought by target audience**

- editor's benefits
- readers' benefits

5 **Quality criteria**

- evidence of relative importance of quality variables:

    - take from Notes for Authors
    - add new points from the critical reading of papers.

List in order of importance, for example: originality, research rigour, practical applications, contribution to body of knowledge, clarity, internationality and others you think count. The reviewers and ultimately the readers of different journals may have slightly different views about what is important. Know this first, or risk coming across the reviewer who wrote:

> The results seem to be presented in a rather curious way, with apparently quite important findings virtually ignored while less satisfactory findings are highlighted.

Quality, as we know by now, is determined by the customer. Take pains to note which contributors to quality this particular customer ranks most highly.

Implications for treatment

How will you meet the objectives and satisfy the needs you have defined above? Try to summarize what you now know into simple statements that show how you will attend to your findings. For example, if rigour of research methodology ranks as the most important variable for a target readership seeking new research approaches, you might write something like this:

Criterion: Research methodology

My plan for approaching the research was ...

I identified my sample group by ...

I tested the sample by ...

I chose to conduct semi-structured interviews because ... and so on.

Alternatively, if the quality of the contribution to the body of knowledge is most important, you will have to emphasize the literature review and therefore might note something like this:

Criterion: Evaluative review of relevant literature

I identified key contributors by ...

I chose the following sources of information ...

Now follow the five points below:

1 **Summarize**. Who said what when? In chronological order or based around key themes, note and describe the work of key figures who have impacted on your area of research.
2 **Synthesize**. Tell the readers how you make sense of what has been written so far. Synthesize the literature after summarizing it, using only a few sentences, as in the example below:

> In short, a gap seems to exist between research results (including normative advice to guide management action) and general product development practice. This can partly be explained by the insufficient diffusion of the results of scientific research. (Biemans and Harmsen, 1995)

3 **Analyse**. Now that you've summarized and made sense of where everyone else has been, what do you think of their progress so far? Your reader will want to know now where you stand. Have there been important flaws thus far in the thinking and work of other people? Did they make a critical error in either their methodology or conclusions? Did they nudge against the frontiers of knowledge but fail to break through for specific reasons?
4 **Authorize**. Enter the expert. That's you. What have you discovered? What has your own empirical research shown you? Where, if you have not conducted empirical research, has your new conceptual thinking brought you?
5 **Interpret and justify**. All your work eventually leads to interpreting and justifying your findings. Make notes about how you will do this. Don't attempt to fake it here. If your findings were not all you expected, say so. If they don't quite prove the point you hoped to make, don't march grimly along your predetermined path. Wave the white flag and tell them how you might get it better next time. Otherwise, you will fall into the trap of so many who are desperate for publication at any cost – trying to fool the reviewer. Don't bother. You don't want to incite the reviewer who said:

> The interpretation of some of the results is heroic bordering on the implausible.

The five points above cover the main issues any author must consider before planning the paper in any more detail. It sets the frame for what is to come and allows you to write a brief synopsis of the paper.

The synopsis

As we're told for computer programming, so we can say for synopses: keep it simple and short. Use the criteria we have already discussed to draw attention to the paper's value to the reader.

As we have discussed in earlier chapters, the paper itself has no inherent value; it is merely a product of the author's making. The only value it has relates to what the readers want.

Discipline yourself to restrict your synopsis to a maximum of two pages. Once you have thought through and made notes on the issues above, it will take a very short time to write 1000 words or so. The following headings will guide you:

- **Target readership**. ('The paper is designed for researchers in the field of applied mathematics who are seeking innovative approaches')
- **Statement of aims**. ('The paper focuses on the problem currently faced by researchers and shows how, using a new approach, some of the obstacles are removed')
- **Implications**. ('The paper reveals how researchers can use the new technique in the following circumstances to obtain the desired results …')
- **Treatment**. ('The paper will be 6000 words long and cover the following sections in this order: introduction, background, evaluative review of relevant literature, method, review of method, findings, analysis, implications, conclusions, references')
- **Availability**. ('The paper will be ready for delivery to the journal in three weeks')
- **Author(s)**. ('The authors are professor and senior lecturer respectively at the University of West London, whose research has been funded by the Institute of Applied Mathematics. Please see brief biographical details attached')

The synopsis can now act as your guide for creating the detailed outline to follow and to circulate to joint authors and other colleagues. It sets clearly the intent and value of the paper and demonstrates that the hard homework of preparation is finished. In the order above, it also demonstrates that you have thought through the paper from the reader's perspective and have successfully matched the reader's needs with your own needs and resources.

You can find out whether or not an editor wants a synopsis by checking the Notes for Authors. More often than not, the editor will want to see the completed paper in preference to a synopsis. After all, if you have done your research on the journal, it should be obvious that the paper is, in principle, suitable. This can reassure you that the paper will meet the first objective of sending it to a journal: getting it into the review stream.

The synopsis and the key points above are critical for your own clarity. There is, after all, no fear of confused writing if the thinking is clear.

In Chapter 11 we explore how to create the template for the writing to come. This is the detailed outline which will guide you effortlessly to your word processor with no fear of writer's block.

Summary

This chapter began by stating that an academic paper could be finished in a week. It may take authors several weeks to research adequately the target journal and work through the questions posed earlier. This is not, of course, weeks of doing nothing else. I assume that the author will integrate the process of finding journals and reading them into daily working life. But, once you have sat down and summarized the relevant information into a synopsis you can look at the calendar and plan how you will celebrate in a week's time. Indeed, like most well prepared authors, you will realize that the writing itself takes a fraction of the preparation time.

Any activity that appears effortless, whether it's ice-skating, opera or writing, only gives that impression because of the training and preparation that preceded the event. Abraham Lincoln's famous Gettysburg Address – the 'government of the people, by the people, and for the people' – lasted less than two minutes. The speaker who preceded him at Gettysburg, Edward Everett, talked for two hours. Does anyone remember him? Does anyone remember what he said?

Action points

This chapter has given numerous suggestions for ways to bring your paper to draft form. Why not review them today and start making notes? That way, you will have on file all the important questions and answers about the journal, editor, reviewers and readers. No author could ask for a more complete picture of the market and how to satisfy it.

11 Writing the draft

Your work has now prepared you for sketching and filling in your outline for the paper. This should now be a straightforward task. You know what you will write and how you will write it. In other words, you have a clear idea of what your article needs to be accepted and know exactly how to achieve it. Indeed, you may choose to use this chapter as your own work plan for actually writing the article. We're only working on the first draft here, so don't worry whether or not every word is right. There's time for that later.

An outline is not there to restrict you, only to guide your thinking and writing. As you proceed, you may well add new points or decide you have already spent too much time on one point. It's a little like going on a motoring holiday; you need a map to be sure you finally reach your destination, but there's no harm in taking the occasional diversion if it seems right at the time. When writing your draft take the opportunity to add notes liberally in each section. In the next chapter we will see how to transform those first draft notes into clear, readable prose.

Journal articles vary in required length, from short pieces of 1000 words or so to long articles and monographs of 12 000 words or more. The requirements of the journal and the quality criteria they are seeking will also vary. So, what do they have in common? Is there any definitive structure or approach that can be applied to all? Yes. The basic rules of communication will apply no matter who the audience and what the format.

Sensible structure

Every article should have a beginning, a middle and an end, evident to the reader. En route through the article, the reader needs to know not only what is being said at the time, but where it's leading to. There is much current debate on the Internet about what style and procedural guidelines writers using that medium should adopt. As the number of electronic journals and newsgroups increase, a feeling is growing that a new, more individualistic and idiosyncratic style is acceptable. Opinions vary, and readers of this book will no doubt have their own. My personal bias is that any communication's objective is to achieve understanding with the reader. The more idiosyncratic we become the more barriers we may raise. Using a modem or a printer is only a choice of form, not of content. Musicians who play different instruments still use the same scales. My final cautionary note is to remind you that people who become too self-conscious of their personal style begin to lose respect for the reader's needs. (See References on page 139 for some Internet sites where this topic has been aired in some detail.)

Back to basics

There's a mnemonic used in copywriting circles that has successfully guided writers for decades, namely AIDA: Attention, Interest, Desire, Action. Good academic papers follow the same steps. The first sentence does not always have to be a multisyllabic, dull description of what the paper is about. Capture your reader's attention, build interest in what you are saying, encourage them to want to know more and show them what they can do about it next.

This is how one author, writing in the *Journal of Law and Society*, chose to wake up his readers with the first line of his paper on law and social theory:

> An economist who talks about unified theory to lawyers and social scientists gets welcomed rather like the British expedition to Afghanistan in 1840. (Cooter, 1995)

Interested? Of course we are. Because we are intrigued, we will read on. What do we ask at this point? 'Tell me why this comparison works and what it means to me.' If the author is skilful enough to sustain our interest, he or she will inspire us to learn more about the subject and, ultimately, encourage us to undertake research or practical activity in the form the author describes at the end of the article.

The foolproof guide to sketching a good draft is to put yourself in the reader's place and to hear the questions he or she is asking. If you know what they are asking now and anticipate what they are about to ask, you will be able to answer their questions as you move through your paper. Two particular questions will prevail:

- What does this mean? (What does this phrase mean? What is this strange language? What is this technique the author is describing?)
- So what? (Why was this technique important? Why did the author choose to refer so extensively to this literature? What is the most important finding? How will it affect the field or me?)

Keep your reader's 'What does this mean?' and 'So what?' questions in mind all the time. One reviewer actually posed the reader's question (which, perhaps, the author in this case was preferring to ignore) when he or she wrote:

> A critical reader would say – 'what's this about?' The answer would be, a rather traditionalist view of power management.

We will now look at each section of a typical academic paper and list the key points to attend to in the outline.

The introduction – the hook

Ask yourself: what is my reader wanting to know? For any paper, any reader will ask the following questions as he or she begins to read it:

- What's this about?   (Attention)
- Is it interesting?   (Interest)
- Should I read it?   (Desire)
- Can I use it?   (Action)

You have roughly 30 seconds of a reader's time to answer those questions. You think you are too busy to write? Readers are too busy to read. With all the other pressures of time and competing interests, you must immediately incite them to carry on reading.

Whether the reader is one of the pre-publication editorial review team or the eventual post-publication consumer, the questions are the same. The reviewer may view the article unfavourably within the first two pages, yet continue to read out of professional obligation. The final reader has no such duty. Two reviewers' comments summarize the importance of a good introduction:

> Introductory section is poorly structured, lacking problem definition.

> Some more effort should be made to think about why the results are interesting. The authors must have had some informal model in mind when they framed their questions. Were they surprised by the answers? I think they should add in one or two paragraphs to spell out what they expected to find. This would then allow them to highlight some results as being particularly interesting.

Imagine you are on a busy street corner and the two people you want to tell about your work are passing on the other side of the street, deep in conversation with each other. What will you do? Mutter quietly, 'You might stop and listen for a minute while I tell you about all the research I've been doing for the last two years' or shout across the traffic, 'Hey! You people don't know half of what you think you know! You! Yes, you! I've worked out the answer! Listen to me and save time, make more money, win more friends!' An introduction must immediately grab attention.

In the introduction you will explain to the reader:

1   the purpose of your paper
2   why it is important
3   to whom it is important
4   what they will discover by reading it.

In the introduction you give the readers the story in a nutshell. You keep back no secrets; you don't let them struggle through 5000 words to discover whether it was all worthwhile. It's an executive summary. You give a glimpse of the end of the story at the beginning. Readers then know what you discovered and why, and now they want to find out how and what really happened.

Think of it as a pyramid shape. Your initial data burst is right at the top. Slowly now, take them down step-by-step where they will learn the detail of what you did and find out how they can apply your findings if they appear as truly credible as you led them to believe. All your practice so far in the 20-words-or-less exercise will have prepared you well for this. By now you know clearly the answers to the four points above and will easily write the first-draft 1000 words in less than two hours.

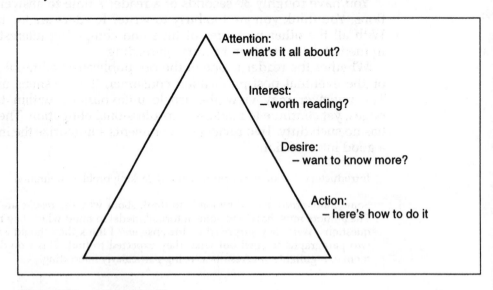

Figure 11.1: AIDA pyramid

Background

What is your reader's next question? They know what your article is about and what it can do for them, they want to find out more, yet something is nagging at the back of their minds – they know you've got something significant to say, but, wait just a minute. Who are you, anyway? What gives you the idea that you can pontificate on such deep and profound matters?

Tell them. Explain who you are and why you tackled the problem. Remind them of the reasons everyone in the field has been searching for answers. In other words, now is the time to back down from the top where you have been shouting like a newly converted religious fanatic and be on the level again. Take your place amongst the rest of us and put your findings or concepts into context. This is a stage of reassurance, of credibility, of common interest. No one wants to feel stupid, although they might not mind feeling briefly provoked. But now that you've provoked them, come back to earth and explain yourself.

If you haven't written a good introduction, you may have lost them by now. Too many academic articles drift through a turgid mass of rationalization and explanation before they say anything of interest. But you haven't done that. You've captured their attention, and now you're building their interest by satisfying their need to be convinced.

This section should be about the same length as your introduction – anywhere between 400 and 1000 words. This, again, is an easy section to write. You know yourself and your research team, you are aware of how the problem came into being and your literature review has yielded enough key people to refer to who shared your problem. Just one note of caution. Be careful not to allow this section to degenerate into self-aggrandisement or the description of detail that you find fascinating but which others may not. Remember the 'So what?' question. The function of this section is solely to lend credibility to what you say and to give some insight and interest to your investigations.

Consider a firm of solicitors. If they wanted to project an image of trustworthiness and expertise, which approach do you think they would best use? 'Our service is great, everyone in this firm is really clever, we all have degrees, we're completely honest, we won't rip you off, and in fact we're the best firm in town'? Or 'For more than ninety years, our firm has advised clients on legal problems. Since developing our specialized personal injuries advice centre in 1959, we have become recognized as the foremost authorities on personal injury legislation in Western Europe. That is why we are able to say with some certainty that if you need the very best advice on a personal injury matter, you should talk, in confidence to …'? One approach is self-focused, the other is oriented towards the users of the service.

By now, you should be able to write this section and, if you choose to do it in one sitting, you could crack another 1000 words in a couple of hours.

The method – the line

Explanation

Now the readers are genuinely interested, but have moved into a more neutral, and potentially critical, phase. What are they asking now? Questions such as: 'OK, I see what you're saying and where you're coming from, but I've been puzzling over the very same questions and haven't found an answer. How did you decide to go about it?' Readers dislike being misled just as did the reviewer who wrote:

> The first, very general, point is that we are told virtually nothing of the research method employed, e.g. why the sample cities were selected, how the data collection was performed, and the time period.

This is where you explain the research programme you undertook because it is here that the reviewer or eventual reader may start to doubt the findings. If you are writing an article based on research already undertaken, such as your own Masters or Doctoral research, by now the methodology is history. If it was truly weak there is nothing you can do about it now except be honest about it and perhaps reformat the presentation of the research in a different way. Another reviewer gave this advice to an author:

> The empirical work is flawed (research design, sample design and measurement evaluations). It would have been more appropriate to report on several focus groups and label this 'exploratory research'.

If you have chosen an unusual methodology, you will have to spend more effort explaining it for the sake of those readers who may not be as familiar with it. The comments below, from reviewers, show how important they find this step:

> As written, the paper is very difficult to follow. A fair knowledge of research methodology in general and conjoint analysis in particular is necessary for comprehending the bulk of the paper.

> Justify the qualitative/quantitative research blend more fully. The approach is sound, but justify your method.

> The empirical work is fully supported by the well-established multivariate methods. One thing is not clear for the reader: why were those specific econometric methods chosen as tools? Those are certainly advanced methods, but perhaps simpler methodology would have been enough to answer the questions, especially in the case of that low response rate. It seems to me that the author wanted to use that methodology in any case.

The important words in the above extract are 'one thing is not clear for the reader'. Note that the reviewer is not dispensing altogether with the author's choice, but demonstrates that the lack of justification and analysis raises certain doubts.

It is now your responsibility to explain how you approached the problem or issue and justify your decisions. Why did you choose to interview those ten people? Why did you choose to use that statistical package? It's too late to go back and redo the research, but perhaps you've planned to carry out more research to justify further your findings. Say so. You have already asked yourself many of these questions when you did your preparation about quality criteria. Now, you have to put the readers' questions to yourself and plan how you will answer them.

Readers' questions at this stage will include:

- What general approach was taken? Why?
- What specific techniques were chosen? Why?
- What commonly-used techniques were not chosen? Why not?
- What limited the author's approach? How were these limitations resolved?

In a classic research student's textbook, *The Management of a Student Research Project* (Howard and Sharp, 1983), the authors gave the following advice to authors of research reports, based on the reader's thought process:

Question–answer

Every time you generate a question – 'But, what is the critical variable?' – the reader will expect an answer to follow quickly.

Problem–solution

When you describe a problem – 'Measuring the effects of training is notoriously difficult' – the reader wants to know what the solution is or, if there is not one, why not.

Cause–effect/effect–cause

Cause and effect – if this, then that – must be linked, in whatever order you present it. One reviewer's comment expanded on this:

> The only problem which I have with the proposed model is characterising it as a 'causal model'. Since there are many other relevant factors involved in product management and they are included in the model, the relationship amongst components cannot be conceptualised as causal relationships. At best, they may be conceptualised as having strong and significant correlation with each other.

General–specific

When making a general or sweeping statement – 'Few researchers know how to approach a literature review' – the reader will want to see how you qualify it with specific examples and evidence. I would also add that the converse is also true. When you make specific statements – 'The researcher learned how to do a literature review' – the reader will want to know what happened so that the comment can be generalized. Adding to the body of knowledge usually requires generalization, but not to the point of obscurity. Along these lines, one reviewer wrote:

> The writing goes from disturbing generality to syrup.

Execution

All that is very well, but your reader is now asking 'So what?' How did your approach work in practice? Now that you've described your methodology, you should explain how it went. This section is not simply descriptive, as in 'We did not interview the number of people we had hoped to, as many were unavailable', but also analytical. What happened and why? The reviewers' comments below emphasize the point:

> Good empirical work, although the qualitative data seems largely ignored … was it collected solely to develop the instrument?

> The results seem to be correct due to the well-established research methodology. My only observation is the low response of the survey that raises questions about the effectiveness of the preliminary steps.

There are implications in your research methodology that you must articulate. If you have not thought these through already, now is the time to review your research method and analyse its limitations in practice. Perhaps you realized halfway through the process that certain weaknesses existed; perhaps you realized this only at the end. Of course, this is not to say that you must be negative. In analysing your approach after the event you may have discovered that a particular method worked better than you had expected, or may have application to other researchers in other fields. This is what your reader wants to know now.

This is a critical phase of your work. This is where you show your ability to reflect on your methodology and offer constructive comments about how you, or others, might approach it differently next time. That you recognize certain weaknesses and discuss them is not called failure, it's called learning. How they affect your results is something that needs to be discussed not first by a sceptical reviewer, but by you.

By contributing in this way to the body of knowledge you are giving other people clear indications of the future. You are sharing your learning and helping them to carry out their work more effectively.

Analysis – the sinker

Here's the big 'So what?' for your reader. You've already given a preview of things to come in your introduction when you briefly outlined your findings. You've described how you approached the problem and what went right and wrong with your approach. Where appropriate, you have indicated how the work of other people has also contributed, or failed to contribute, to the question. Now, your reader is asking how you are reaching your conclusions. Given the evidence, given the theory, what have you done with it?

At this stage, too many people still find themselves in a descriptive mode. They report on their evidence and the literature in a passive, unquestioning way. They are, as many reviewers observe, still at an undergraduate essay-writing level. The only difference between undergraduates and postgraduates, or researchers in non-academic institutions, is that undergraduates are not obliged to add to the body of knowledge. They are only obliged to understand it. You, however, are supposed to be contributing something, developing it and adding to it. You can only do that by being critical.

Make sure, when you report on your data, that you are relating them to the research question at hand. Sometimes, particularly if your methodology has been weak, you may be tempted to simply report upon the findings that look the most interesting to you. But remember the reader. What is going to be interesting and meaningful to your audience? Having worked through the previous chapters of this book, you will by now, of course, have noted the critical implications of your work and analysed them from the reader's perspective. You prepared the reader to expect certain reassurances, and now is the time to give them. Prove yourself here – not in 20 words or less this time – but in depth.

Implications

At this stage, your readers are asking: 'Where are we?' Do not make the mistake here of perceiving a conclusion simply as a reiteration of what you've said already. That's the first part of your concluding statement, not the whole story. Your reader is asking here: 'What does it mean to me?'

If you review your earlier work on implications, you will see that you are now in a good position to pull this section together. Take your previous notes and see how you can expand them. Relate the implications to your previous sections by summarizing the key points of your argument and your findings.

We are not the sum total of our experience. Our learning shows us that our experience or evidence is there to guide us, but it is up to us to take it further. It is here that your readers are looking for your own sense of 'So what?' where they expect, and deserve, to know how what you have learned can apply to them or the greater body of researchers working in the same field. We have done enough work on implications so far not to have to belabour this point. You should be able to write this section clearly and fluidly. Devote up to 20 per cent of the total words to this section.

Review

Now that you have mapped out your paper it's a good idea to return to the introduction to make sure that you have included the main points. Reviewing your introduction ensures that you won't inadvertently miss a point which may have only occurred to you strongly in the body of your paper.

Summary

If you have followed the pattern so far you will have a clear draft. By now, you will have broken through the fear of being unable to write by realizing that it's the planning, not the writing, that makes the difference. Polished writing alone is no substitute for clear planning.

Authors can complete this stage in a few sittings over two or three days. The paper is now seen emerging logically, if not elegantly, and most of the worries about where to start and how have vanished. In Chapter 12, we will examine the principles of good writing.

Action points

Review the points made during this chapter, and work your notes and ideas through to first draft. Don't work on each word or turn of phrase, but concentrate on pulling the whole piece together. If you have taken this step-by-step approach, congratulations. Polishing the draft takes work, but you can be confident now that you have a working document.

12   Points of style

It's time now to refine the paper. If you have prepared yourself along the lines described thus far in this book, you will find you can accomplish the next stages with ease and fluidity. Don't let the easiness of the task fool you into doubting you're on the right track. You have just debunked the writer's block myth, that's all. You've already done the hard work, and you're now about to discover that writing itself is not as difficult as you may have thought when you first approached the idea. Writing is a pleasure, almost effortless, when you are absolutely sure about what you are saying to whom. Now it's time to relax and enjoy yourself.

In this chapter, we will explore how to get the paper right. Many articles have all the makings of a fine paper, but are poorly written. Part of writing well is being able to stand back and look at your work objectively. Difficult as this may be, it becomes easier with practice. In an ideal world, we would all be able to detach ourselves from what we do but, as this is never humanly possible, the best we can do is invite outsiders to look at our finished work. As a first step, these outsiders may be friends and colleagues, but ultimately they will be the reviewers of the chosen journal. Far from being a negative relationship, the relationship with the editor and reviewer should be welcomed and viewed positively.

It's quite a reasonable piece in many ways, but lacks depth. It would be a pity to reject it outright, and discourage the author. It just needs more work!

I would hope that they would consider the points more fundamentally because the general topic is important to the research literature as well as to professionals.

Many reviewers, like the ones quoted above, offer constructive and encouraging advice to authors whose work they perceive as deserving merit and who have obviously taken the time and trouble to target the right journal. Unfortunately, one of the problems editors say they have with authors is persuading them to revise the paper and resubmit it on time. It appears that many authors take a request to revise as a personal insult, almost as a rejection. Nothing could be further from the editor's intention. It would be easy to see the relationship between the author and reviewer as one of opposition. We should, however, regard it as a partnership in which each party is trying to achieve the same goal: communication with the reader to eventually enhance the field of enquiry.

Elements of style

The most common cause of poor style is poor thinking. Muddled thought will always result in a muddled expression. What elements of style do reviewers seek? An analysis of several editorial briefings to reviewers reveals the following points of style summarized by editors:

- literate, clear and well organized
- logically structured
- conclusions matching what is promised at the outset
- economy of style
- sharp focus.

Looking at that list, it's immediately apparent that we have conquered most of those obstacles to poor writing. Your thinking is now clear and reader-focused. Your structure and draft sections reflect your understanding of your reader, your chosen journal and your own understanding of your work. Adhere to the following few principles and your writing will become clear and a pleasure to read. Yet, if clarity and readability are criteria of a good paper, what are its components? How can we be sure we are being clear? This relates to your quality of thinking, as we considered earlier. It will also depend upon your structure and flow of argument. But, even then, there are common pitfalls we can avoid.

Jargon

Jargon is the vocabulary with which we are familiar. It is the turn of phrase, the word, the descriptor that we develop as a means of private shorthand. We know we are familiar with it, our colleagues are familiar with it, but the reader is completely lost.

Read your material carefully and ask yourself whether your readers will understand. If you have any doubt, change the word or phrase into user-friendly language. Examine the concepts that you have borrowed from other people. Have you slipped into using their method of expression? Is it likely that people unfamiliar with their work will understand? Better yet, give your paper to someone who does not work with you but may have a general interest in the field. Does this person stumble upon words or phrases he or she does not understand?

Most journals, however specialized, are unwilling to accept articles only decipherable by a small group of specialists. Their Notes for Contributors normally specify this requirement, but even if they do not, authors should take it as a given. The guidance notes for even a highly specialized journal, *Bioscience*, are unequivocal:

> Articles should review significant scientific findings in an area of interest to a wide range of biologists. They should include background for biologists in disparate fields. The writing should be free of jargon.

Big words

Words are there to convey meaning, to express – not to impress. The best writing is always the simplest and the clearest. When you use a word of three syllables or more, check yourself. Is there really a good reason to use that longer word? The best way to avoid using the wrong word is to keep your words as simple as possible. Use your dictionary, but throw away your thesaurus. Too often, people consult a thesaurus to find a bigger, more important-sounding word for the more common, more familiar word. If you are going to use a thesaurus, use it the other way round, to move from the complex to the simple.

Wrong words

Are you sure about the meaning of the words you use? Did you know that transpire doesn't mean 'happen' but 'become known'? That 'enervate' means 'lack of energy', not 'enthusiasm'? That irregardless, being a double negative, means 'with regard to'? Are you sure about accept/except, affect/effect, illusion/allusion, infer/imply? Do you use 'over' when you should use 'more than'? Are you confused about principles and principals? There are many excellent books currently available that describe some of the most common misused words and are excellent guides to style. The best general advice is to remain vigilant. Whenever you have even the whisper of a doubt in your own mind, check the word or phrase. There's an old but true cliché in publishing: when in doubt, leave it out.

Most journals today are international; we must therefore assume that readers will have, as their mother tongues, languages other than our own. Knowing that, authors of any nationality must avoid using idioms and colloquialisms that may not be familiar to other readers. Indeed, it is always poor style to put quotation marks around a word or expression from which you want to distance yourself. If you don't want to use the word, don't use it.

Misspelled and missing

No points here for lack of care. Use a dictionary constantly. Your computer spell-check is good, but not infallible.

When I first began reading reviewers' reports, I was surprised by the number of times those overworked people had to go back to primary school level and tell the author about basic spelling. It astonished me that anyone considering publication had not spent the extra time proofing their work. Still, and perhaps even more surprisingly, reviewers patiently send back reports like these:

> Page 16: (2nd para) The third line appears to be mis-typed.

> Page 5: para 2: 'interested' is misspelt.

Once again, previous points about proofreading need emphasis here. Don't trust yourself. Have more than one other person read through it carefully. Take their advice. If something you have said is not clear to your reader, don't bother explaining it face-to-face. It simply hasn't worked. Rewrite it. It once took me two or three rereadings to spot a typographical error in my own work that may have transformed the way people approached conventional business strategy. The standard four components of a SWOT analysis (Strengths, Weaknesses, Opportunities and Threats) had appeared as: strengths, weaknesses, opportunities and treats. In another example, it took a sub-editor to see that an article that began discussing 'winning teams' later referred to 'sinning teams'. We should not leave the potential to revisit standard theory to the whims of imperfect typists.

Proofreading our own work is dangerous. After all, we know what we think we are saying, so that's what we tend to read.

Punctuation

Punctuation is there to aid comprehension. Standard style books can help if you still haven't worked out the difference between colons, semi-colons, full stops and commas. A good rule of thumb is: the more you resort to punctuation as a device, the less well structured your sentences tend to be. Put the thinking into your sentence structure and you'll find you will need little extra.

Use dashes and parentheses sparingly. That's not to say that they are never required, but you should develop the habit of working harder at the sentence structure itself. Compare these two sentences:

'There are many variables (cost, quality, location, promotion) which affect the customer's decision to shop at any one retail outlet.'

'Cost, quality, location and promotion all affect the customer's decision ...'

Use a style guide if you become confused with plurals and possessives: its, it's, readers', reader's.

Exclamation marks are seldom appropriate in academic style. Certainly, they cannot be used to indicate humour or amazement. If this is your intention, choose your words and phraseology to communicate the meaning. Adding an exclamation mark to the end of the sentence will not revive a flagging joke.

Abbreviations and acronyms

Again, use sparingly. You may know what MPRP stands for, but your reader may not. Spell out Manuscript Proofing and Revision Process (MPRP) and put the initials in parentheses. It is generally preferable to always use the full phrase rather than the acronym.

Put a red mark through every 'etc'. If you can't think of something else to say, finish the sentence. Etc., while occasionally helpful, frequently indicates the trailing off of a lazy or tired mind and is usually inappropriate in academic writing.

If you want to say 'for example' say it, rather than 'e.g.'. If you want to say 'that is' then say so, rather than 'i.e.'. And don't, for example, confuse the two. They are not synonymous.

Unfailingly, thinking through what you are saying will help you avoid needless or confusing abbreviations.

Metaphors and clichés

Be careful. Most metaphors are so overused that they have lost their original freshness. Worse, many are mixed and not logically followed. You don't want to be down the creek without a paddle only to find you are shooting for the stars. Ask yourself: can I find a real example for this? Can I describe what I am saying in a vivid way?

Clichés can be bought from the same department. You don't even have to think about them. Unfortunately, people use them so often that your mind will quite readily offer them to you without any effort. That, naturally, is the problem.

The easiest way to guard against metaphors and clichés is simply to become aware of how effortlessly you are writing. If the words are flowing on to the page without any reference to your brain, you can bet your bottom dollar that your mind has turned to putty and you're flying like a bird. Land. Reread. Revise.

Economy

Why take 200 words to say something when 50 will do? As one reviewer observed:

> The entire page could be boiled down to one or two statements.

Go back to your plan. If you originally thought the section was only going to need 200 words, why are you still writing after 750? Most probably, it's because you've become carried away by your own thoughts and lost touch with what the reader needs. You may have become unsure of what you are trying to say, so you keep avoiding coming to a conclusion.

Of course, that isn't to say that there are times when the plan was not precisely right. Perhaps, now you've begun the process you've realized you underestimated the length required. Perhaps, but not likely. Most of the mistakes authors make occur through poor planning, lack of focus and absence of a clear structure. Have faith in what you have already worked out. Discipline yourself to write less than you want. At worst, you may have to go back and insert an extra line or two, but you'll find that much easier than having to reduce four pages of waffle to two paragraphs. Reviewers, much less readers, are unimpressed by long, turgid sentences. Keep it short, keep it simple.

Descriptors

Descriptors are adjectives or adverbs, or compound phrases incorporating adverbs and adjectives. While it is neither necessary nor desirable to eliminate all descriptors, too often they are a substitute for a more precise noun or verb. Too many of them lead to a dull paper, or a paper so padded with extra words that the reader begins to suspect the author of waffle. For example, substitute 'very, very, good' with 'outstanding' and 'a richer range' with 'variety'. Remember:

> The adjective hasn't been built that can pull a weak or inaccurate noun out of a tight place. (Strunk and White, 1979)

Tone

The tone in an academic journal is said to be 'formal.' What does that mean? The easiest way to understand this is to relate tone to everyday speech. Most of us will tend to speak differently amongst our family and friends than with our clients and bosses. In a casual setting we let our words tumble out and take it for granted that our friends will understand us. Most of the time, given our background of familiarity, we will be right. Our friends don't mind when we say 'Wanna coffee?' but a stranger visiting our office would expect to be asked, in a more formal tone, 'Would you like a cup of coffee?'. One is casual, or informal, and the other is formal.

In much the same way, we are writing for a group of people we have never met. We cannot assume familiarity with our particular affectations of speech. To do so may obscure meaning. We therefore revert to our common language, our common structure. We obey rules of grammar, although we may not in everyday speech. Our objective is to be understood, not to be regarded affectionately as an eccentric.

The best guide to tone is the journal you are targeting. If you look at the *Harvard Business Review* you will find articles with such titles as 'What the heck is wrong with our leaders these days?' or words of a similar tone. This would be inappropriate for many other journals which would prefer something along the lines of 'An analysis of leadership performance factors'.

One feature of tone is the active or passive voice. The active voice is more clear and fresh – 'Wax brightens floors' – whereas the passive voice is quieter and less excited – 'Floors are brightened by wax'. Another advantage of the active voice is that it enhances meaning. The closer the verb to the subject, the easier it is to understand what the author is saying. Consider the two examples below:

'People have always been, with the exception of a few in the southern regions, and not forgetting the influence of the weather, inclined to eat a hot meal in the evening.'

'Eating a hot meal in the evening is common practice for people living in the north. Those in more southerly regions prefer their hot meals in the middle of the day, as do many northerners when the weather is hot.'

In the first example the reader has to read 24 words to discover what 'people have always been ...'. In the second, the point is stated immediately.

Most computer programs have a grammar check which, while ponderous, points out the passive sentence. We don't want all our writing to be the same, and some journals will tend to be more passive than others, but it's good discipline to double-check every sentence.

Positivity

Try to write in positive statements. It is verbose, and sometimes pompous, to express yourself in the negative voice. 'A not inconsiderable investment of time was involved' should be expressed 'A great deal of time was invested'. Rather than 'The research results did not appear on time', write 'The research results were late'. Attune your ear to the use of 'not' and try to avoid it.

Manuscript presentation

Examine each journal for specific style points. You will have noted this already when working through Chapter 9 on targeting journals, but you must review your findings when you put the final touches to your manuscript.

How does the journal treat footnotes? Does it have a preferred minimum and maximum number of references? Which reference system does it use? How should figures, tables and illustrations be presented? Does the journal make a charge for colour photographs or detailed mathematics?

The manuscript's presentation is the first indication to an editor or reviewer whether or not the paper has been properly targeted. Perhaps the journal states that all references should be numbered sequentially in the text, but yours are presented alphabetically. The journal might state that footnotes and cross-referencing within the text should be used sparingly, and you have nearly six pages in which the footnotes take up most of the page. Why make it so difficult for the editor or reviewer to judge your work favourably?

Professor Harry Dickinson, editor of *History*, advises authors to select the appropriate journal carefully and then says, 'Please look at the journal's housestyle and follow it to the best of your ability – it is such a relief to the editor and gives a good initial impression'.

Consult the Notes to Authors in the journal itself. Some are more detailed than others, depending on the journal. *The Chicago Manual of Style* is often referred to in journals' guidance notes. It provides useful sections on style and form.

As a minimum, all manuscripts must:

- be typed double-spaced on single sides of A4
- have stapled and numbered pages
- include a cover page with the paper's title and names of author(s), affiliations and addresses
- include an abstract.

Normally – and this is where you must consult the individual journal's Notes for Authors – you will also be asked to:

- send three copies
- include a running head or footer with title and author on each page
- include a version of your manuscript on disk according to the journal's specification.

The rest of the presentation must accord with the specific journal requirements. For example, *Psychophysiology*, the international journal of the Society for Psychophysiological Research, offers strict guidance for authors on what to include on the first four pages of the manuscript and how to structure the rest of the paper. A separate guidance note on how to approach critiques and replies is supplied upon request. This demonstrates the considerable lengths a journal editor and publisher will go to for the sake of prospective authors.

Writing an abstract

An abstract is a short summary of your article, which contains all the key points it makes. Abstracts are normally printed at the head of the article they refer to, or all together on an abstracts page.

An abstract's purpose is to tell browsers, searchers and indexers what a paper contains. It should attract a reader who seeks a particular kind of information or approach. Just as importantly, it should deter a reader who is seeking specific information which is not in your article. The function is, therefore, not to 'sell' your article to all and sundry, but to indicate its usefulness to the people who will benefit from reading it. It is, once again, a question of targeting your audience properly and delivering your promise.

How can you digest all your discussion into, typically, less than a hundred words? Using the following technique, distilled from professional abstractors, you can do this quickly, easily and informatively, in just three sentences.

Sentence one: the purpose

The first sentence of your abstract should restate the purpose of the paper. Abstractors say that the abstract should normally start with a verb rather than 'This paper …', which is redundant. Try verbs such as: discusses, argues, suggests, shows, studies, reviews, and so on.

For example, an abstract for this book might have as its first sentence: 'Shows how prospective authors can prepare publishable papers for learned journals.'

Sentence two: the argument

This sentence summarizes the main points of your argument and the methodology you used. How did you show, discuss, demonstrate? Select the main points of your argument for inclusion.

The second sentence of this book's abstract might read: 'Presents a series of frameworks which discuss, *inter alia*, selecting a prospective journal, understanding the editorial review process, structuring a paper and writing the paper, drawn largely from research studies and interviews.'

Sentence three: the conclusions

The third sentence summarizes what you have found. What are your main conclusions? What are some of the implications you have revealed?

The third sentence of this book's abstract might read: 'Concludes that, by following the steps and preparation described, an author can turn research and ideas into a publishable paper in a few days.'

Following this simple framework allows you to create an informative abstract for the readers of your paper, quickly and easily. And that's just one more small step towards keeping a journal's editor and publishers happy. Another link in the relationship publishing chain, in fact.

Setting the pace

Taking all of the above into consideration means authors can approach their papers with confidence. The notes on style can serve as a useful checklist to review the first draft. Of course, these are only general rules that are sometimes broken: Chapter 14 discusses how to develop a more personal style and how to develop the habit of good writing.

People who are unaccustomed to writing sometimes make the best writers because they approach the task with a clear goal and a helpful pinch of humility. The author who has prepared the paper's detailed outline and notes, based on the principles discussed so far, can easily write an article in two or three days.

Each time you sit at the word processor, consider it a session. Limit any session to two hours, even if you feel the energy to write more. Two hours is long enough for anyone to concentrate. It's far healthier, and more professional, to take a break, give a lecture, go for a walk, have a cup of coffee, or go to a meeting, and then return to the work refreshed. People who say they cannot write a paper because they can't put time aside over two or three full working days are making excuses. No one sits down to write non-stop for three days. A glance at the biographies of famous writers consistently reminds us that discipline is their key to success, not torment. Most writers deliberately limit themselves to either two hours between breaks, or to a certain number of words per session.

Writing one or two thousand words per session will mean that three or four sessions are required to write an average paper. Authors can easily spread such sessions over three days without ruining their lives. Personally, I always cringe when I read the acknowledgement section of a book or thesis and find sentences that apologize to the author's friends, family and children for being such a terrible person for the past weeks, months or even years. Doesn't the author know how to organize himself or herself? Most likely, they are the sort of would-be author who sits down at a blank screen without first planning what to say, and then screams at everyone else not to disturb the work of a genius.

Good work is done in manageable portions. Getting out of bed an hour earlier or locking the office door for two hours now and then isn't too much to ask. Staring into space and panicking about how to start is a miserable, and largely ineffective, way to spend one's time. But surely, by now, we are all beyond that.

Once the paper is finished allow another week or so to pass while other people have a chance to read it and offer comment. Accept constructive criticism with good grace and amend where you can. The point of the exercise is not to get it right first time, but to get it right enough to subject it to detailed scrutiny by colleagues and friends.

In the next chapter we investigate what has often been referred to as a 'black hole' – that place that papers go when they leave the author's desk on the way to an editor's. What can you expect, and how much can you influence?

Action points

Well, you are just about there. Follow the guidelines given in this chapter. Pay particular attention to your style and language:

- Have you used short words in short sentences in short paragraphs, in preference to long words in long sentences in long paragraphs?
- Have you used any jargon words? If so, reconsider.
- Have you used unexplained acronyms? If so, spell them out. And, remember, if your paper is littered with many different acronyms, even explained, it will be hard to read.
- Have you broken up your text with headings and subheadings? As a rule, you should have a heading per page. If not, go back and add some. They make your manuscript visually more attractive and easier to read.
- Have you checked your spelling? If so, go and do it again anyway.
- Has someone else read through your paper? If not, now is a good time to ask a friend or colleague for 20 minutes of their time. Ask them to indicate clearly any parts they do not understand immediately.

13   Managing the process

Once the paper is finished, copied and checked one last time, it is ready to be sent to the editor. Always enclose a covering letter stating your name, the title of the paper, brief paragraph describing the contents and referring, if possible, to why you chose the specific journal. If there has been previous correspondence relating to a synopsis or a telephone call, refer to it and to any further guidance from the editor which was given at that time.

What happens next, what can you expect, and how can you influence the process, if at all? There are certain well-defined stages through which any paper travels from receipt by editor to publication and receipt by readers. Some depend on the author's involvement, others can be helped by the author's involvement and a few can be hampered by it.

The review process

Stage one: in the post

Yes, post. Faxed papers, unless they are specifically requested in that form, are a nuisance. They eat up the fax roll, they can become mixed up with other faxes, they curl at the edges and all too often transmission fails and the whole process has to start again. The manuscript, even if it is addressed to the editor, will often first be opened by a secretary or editorial assistant. The details from your covering letter will sometimes be logged onto an electronic system for future correspondence.

What can you expect next? At the very least, you should receive an acknowledgement saying that your paper has been received. Many editors will read their papers in batches, every few days or once a week. It may therefore be up to two weeks before a decision is made whether or not to send the paper for review. Depending on how busy the editor is, whether or not she or he is away, or the current backlog, your acknowledgement letter will either tell you that the manuscript is awaiting the editor's attention or it will tell you that the paper has been sent into the review process. As you already know by now, many papers are instantly rejected because they do not conform to the journal's editorial objectives – yours, at least, should not receive this treatment.

Stage two: in for review

A paper that obviously meets the journal's editorial objectives will most likely be reviewed either by the editor, by specialist editors or by one, two or sometimes three members of the review board. In the case of a fully-refereed journal the process is, as discussed earlier, double-blind. It is likely to take between eight and 12 weeks for full articles, and considerably less for reports or short reviews.

The reviewers' comments are sent back to the editor, either on a specially prepared pro forma or on the manuscript itself, accompanied by a report.

It is reasonable to ask for feedback if you have not heard from the editor within 12 weeks. When my organization, the Buckingham Consortium, was asked to create an electronic manuscript tracking system for editors within MCB University Press we asked a core group of editors to identify the vulnerabilities in their own systems. Not hearing back from reviewers swiftly enough was one; not hearing back from authors with their revisions was another. It therefore may be prudent to gently remind the editor that you are still awaiting feedback. That message might prompt the editor to remind the reviewer and therefore help nudge the manuscript along.

Stage three: the judgement

There are only three choices open to the editor having received the reviewer's recommendations. One is to accept the paper as it is, subject to in-house sub-editing. The second is to ask the author to revise the paper in view of the reviewer's comments. The third is to reject it outright.

Acceptance

Acceptance of a paper still might mean that minor changes are required, but these will be made by the editorial staff and will amount to little more than tidying up small sections of writing or changing headings to conform with house style. By implication, if not by direct comment in the Notes for Authors, every journal reserves this right.

Once your paper is accepted you will receive a letter telling you so and an indication of which issue will carry your paper. This date may not be absolutely fixed. Too many articles in a previous issue may result in some papers being held over into the next, or in-house production or print problems may delay the scheduled date.

Some journals work to longer timescales than others, depending on the subject matter and the backlog. If it irks you to think that your paper might not appear for a year after it has been accepted, think again about the length of the review process and consider carefully whether you are prepared to risk more time and potential rejection by another journal. The editor is usually the best judge on these matters. He or she doesn't want an outdated paper in the journal any more than you do. If the editor feels the paper will still have relevance and weight in a year's time, then he or she is usually right.

Rejection

A rejected paper means that the editor and reviewers do not feel it could be appropriate for the readership even if amendments were made. While it is easy to imagine that rejection is purely a function of overload, the truth is somewhat different. Even if an editor has sufficient copy for the next volume, an excellent paper may still be accepted, even if the publication date is further away. The reviewers have no idea what the editor's backlog is, or even if there is one. They merely judge a paper on its merit.

A rejected paper tells you that:

- your paper was badly targeted
- your paper was badly written, badly structured, badly argued, or valueless
- your paper was good, but just not as good as some of the others.

We must assume now that, if you have done your research properly, targeted the journal correctly, structured your article, written it well and followed the journal's Notes for Authors, only the latter could possibly apply. In this case, you should find another journal with a similar readership but with a lower profile and therefore fewer competing submissions.

Revision

Being asked to revise an article is a compliment. It means that you are regarded as a potential contributor to the journal and therefore also as a potential contributor to the body of knowledge. Perhaps all that is missing are a few more references, or a better explanation of your method, or a restructuring to achieve the right emphasis for the journal. Whatever the reason, the reviewers and editors feel you are worth the effort.

You should view this process as not simply extra work but as extra, free, support and advice. Everything the editors and reviewers are doing is in your best interests and the best interests of the field. At this point, everyone is working together for the benefit of other scholars and interested readers. As one reviewer commented:

> It's quite a reasonable piece in many ways, but lacks depth. It would be a pity to reject it outright, and discourage the author. It just needs more work!

It would be easier for them to reject your paper outright. No doubt there are many more like you whose work may be acceptable as it stands. But, rather than reject you, they have decided to work with you to help you amend the article and make it better. The following quotation is one I have reread many times, simply because it shows how much a dedicated reviewer is prepared to give to a willing author:

> I have read this paper several times and, with the best will in the world, it cannot possibly be published in its current form. The argument is very badly structured, the contextual material is almost non-existent and the methodology is very poorly (albeit exhaustively!) explained. To be truthful, the manuscript is almost unintelligible as it stands.
>
> That said, there is the kernel of a useful paper here. ... The author would do well to attempt to approach his/her material from the reader's perspective.

'Almost unintelligible' is not a phrase that anyone wants to hear, but bear in mind that the reviewer still thinks something good might come of it all. Note that the problem in understanding has not come from the words themselves, but the lack of purpose and structure. If you have worked through the previous chapters, you will be unlikely to receive a critique like the above, but even so it does give pause for thought.

How much easier it would have been for the reviewer to simply have recommended rejection; there would be little argument about the justice in that decision. Instead, the reviewer has spent time looking more deeply into the paper's potential and, by virtue of that decision, into the author's potential. Ask experienced authors what it is they value most in the publishing process and the answer will most often be one word: feedback. As experienced and proficient as they may be, they know they can always do better and are grateful for the insights of others who will help them improve their ability to communicate with their audience.

Unfortunately, less experienced and less wise authors can create unnecessary trouble for an editor. Once an article is marked 'revise' it will be sent back to you with an invitation to revise it within a certain period of time. What should you do then?

First, accept the comments with enthusiasm. Respond to the editor immediately agreeing to make the suggested revisions by the date given. Then, without fail, stick to it. But what if you can't? What if the comments are too fundamental to be corrected simply by rewriting parts of the paper? This is not usually the case, simply because papers which are so seriously flawed due to their original methodology or lack of evidence are usually rejected. Sometimes, the reviewer or editor suggests that such a paper can be reduced to a research note, or a report on work in progress.

Revisions are therefore changes that the reviewer thinks you can make based on his or her understanding of your work so far. But, what if that judgement is wrong? What if there is nothing you can do to enhance the parts which were considered weak? Maybe the reviewer hoped you had more information which you could add to your findings, but you don't. Perhaps you glossed over the implications mainly because, upon reflection, you realized your research was so narrow and inconclusive that the findings could not be generalized or applied elsewhere.

Resist making these assumptions before talking to someone else – your supervisor, or another close colleague. Make sure you are not being over defensive and explore deeply the critique you have received in light of all the material you have available. If, after all that, you conclude that you do not have the material available to revise the paper, then say so. Partially revising a paper which has been reviewed is worse than not revising it at all. The impression the incomplete work gives is that either you did not understand the revisions requested or you could not be bothered to make them. In either case, it does nothing to enhance your reputation as a serious researcher.

The best response now is to write back to the editor and explain the problem. Agree with the reviewer's comments, but point out why and where you are unable to make the revisions. Suggest an alternative: perhaps a shorter research note, or a more narrow paper focusing just on the literature, or a report on work in progress if your research is still live. The editor may reject all these ideas, but at least you have given the journal another opportunity.

Some authors at this stage choose to ignore the serious problems being noted on their manuscript and send the paper to another journal hoping that the editors and reviewers there may not notice or care. This is work that should have been done while you were targeting the journals in the first place, given that some journals will put greater or less emphasis on different quality criteria. As you had decided already that your chosen journal was the most suitable, you must ask yourself why you are not able to meet its requirements. The serious problem with sending a poor paper elsewhere is that you might be unlucky enough to get it published. Now, all your flaws and inconsistencies are not being only noticed by an editor and two reviewers but also by everyone else! Far better to reduce the paper to something else if you can, eliminating entirely the unrecoverable sections, and continue your research.

If you are in the position to revise, then do it on time. There are no excuses allowable for authors who agree to meet deadlines and then don't. Saying you are busy is an insult to busy editors and reviewers. Upon entering the review process you made an implicit agreement to accept the judgement of the panel. They have done their job in carefully reading your work and offering you the best critique they can. Now it's your responsibility to take those comments and revise your work according to their advice and schedule.

Once you send your paper back to the editor it will be reviewed again. Sometimes your revisions will adequately reflect their expectations and sometimes they will ask you to go even further. The same principles as we discussed above apply: do your best to respond to their requests, and tell them you are doing so.

Stage 4: into production

Once your manuscript has been accepted by the editorial board it will enter the production process. Nowadays, many publishers work from the disks that the author supplies, or scan from a clean typescript. The manuscript must be reformated into the journal's house style, the figures, tables and illustrations brought into the correct format and the whole paper checked for any errors which were not caught by the author or reviewers. The paper may be edited slightly for style or for length.

The people who do these jobs are sub-editors, proofreaders and typesetters. They are not subject matter experts, nor are they expected to be. As publishing has moved towards a more electronic process, some of the roles overlap.

Sub-editors

Sub-editors are valued for their language and presentation skills. They can usually be trusted to pick up awkward turns of phrase, grammatical problems or spelling mistakes. This is a great help for authors writing in a language which is not their mother tongue. They also check for consistencies within the manuscript, ensuring that if you refer to a diagram, it is there, and it has the same title in the text as it does on the graphic; that references you cite in the text are listed at the end and in the right style; that the people to whom you refer have their names spelled correctly and so on. They also mark up the manuscript for house style, indicating headings, subheadings, indents and other typographical detail. Nowadays, as more publishers incorporate information technology, the sub-editing process is moving from paper to screen. This saves time and money, as fewer errors appear and reappear through rekeying.

Proofreaders

The proofreading function may be taken on by sub-editors as well, or there may be people appointed for just that job. The proofreader reads the final text for typographical errors and double-checks for consistency. If the sub-editor has done the sub-editing job first, then the proofreader should not be checking for style, but rather for mistakes. Proofreading is a science and an art. Training and extensive practice are required to develop the skills of spotting sometimes small mistakes that can be overlooked at first glance.

Typesetters

In the past, typesetters rekeyed the manuscript from the paper version sent by an author. Now, most work from disks supplied by authors. These would normally have been through the sub-editing function first, changed on disk, and then sent through to the typesetters to be put into the final format for the specific issue being produced.

Author's proofs

Authors and editors are usually sent proofs of their papers. The purpose of this is to allow the author to see the final version, and check for typographical errors, but not to make extensive changes. Many publishers will charge the author for any changes made beyond typographical errors. They assume, correctly, that having been through review and possibly revision, the author and editorial board are satisfied with the paper as it stands.

The author is asked to see the proofs mainly because he or she is the best expert on the paper and may catch an error which went unnoticed by the production team. Also, the author's paper may have been edited and it is a courtesy to allow the author to see the changes. It is not, however, expected that the author will disagree with those changes unless a serious problem in understanding has arisen.

Many authors find this stage exceedingly difficult. Each time you see your work you will be tempted to change it. You will think that you could always write a little more clearly; there is always a sentence you think could be improved; there is always something more you think you can say. Of course, you are right. There is always something more. But, remember the advice we heard earlier. There are perfect papers, and there are published papers. Authors must discipline themselves to let their work go.

Some publishers send authors a checklist for proofing. The main points to watch for are inconsistencies:

- Are the authors' names spelled correctly?
- Is the title of the paper correct and is it the same wherever it appears, such as on the title page and on the abstract?
- Is the institution correct?
- Are all the figures, tables, illustrations included? Are they correct? This is often the weak point in the production process, as it is easy to transpose figures or even the axes of graphs.

- Are figures labelled in the text as Figure 1, and so on, and does each figure have the correct label?
- Are references cited in the text listed at the end?
- Are the names of those referenced spelled correctly and consistently?
- Are footnotes correctly labelled and in the right place?

Authors are normally given only a few days to check their proofs and send them back to the publisher. Publishers will not want to delay a whole journal issue because they are awaiting proofs from one author, so as usual the deadline must be met. Some publishers only want the amended pages returned, sometimes by fax.

Summary

This is nearly the end of the story. By now, you should have a clear idea of how to be published. You know that the most important parts precede writing the paper – that the quality of your preparation determines the quality of the finished paper. The skills described in this book have worked for thousands of authors and will work for you. But now, just before you close the book and consider yourself fully skilled, there's something else I want to tell you about.

Action points

There's a fine line between showing understandable enthusiasm and intrusive pestering. Unless a journal's Notes for Authors clearly state the expected review time, you are quite entitled to ask an editor how long you would be expected to wait before receiving a decision on your paper. If you have some kind of pressing deadline, such as a holiday scheduled for six weeks' or a month's time, then do say so. An editor may or may not be able to accommodate you, but at least he or she will know.

If you have submitted a paper and have had no acknowledgement within a couple of weeks, make enquiries. Has the paper been received? Mail can go astray, especially in large institutions, where many editors are based, or if a publisher is forwarding papers to an editor.

If you have been assured that you will hear within a month, and six weeks has now passed, a friendly telephone call or note should not be badly received. Again, the best manuscript tracking systems can break down sometimes. If, however, you have been told that the review process normally takes three months, don't call every week to see 'how it's getting on'. Your careful relationship management work can all be destroyed if an editor believes that he or she is being pestered. They are only human after all.

14   Not by analysis alone

Every other day I work out in the swimming pool of my local gym. It's an arduous programme, intentionally so because my life as a writer and teacher tends to be sedentary and I feel compelled to work my muscles before they decide not to work for me. But, over time, I have developed a knack which keeps me enthusiastically returning for the next session. I play.

I learned to do that because I found the last five laps or so always seemed so tedious that I began to dread the whole experience. The last laps were the final phase of the work-out, and they weren't particularly pleasant. By then, I was tired and a little fed up. So, one day, I decided to relax a little and experiment with different strokes and styles. Now, I incorporate my non-standardized final laps into my regular routine. Sometimes I just float for a while and watch the light shimmer on the wooden ceiling; sometimes I pretend I'm a jellyfish and let my limbs dangle under the water. It's all very silly and unproductive, but I have noticed that other regular swimmers tend to do the same. We do the hard work, diligently, but we also allow ourselves to splash around, or float, or dive, or invent odd little patterns that lighten the routine.

This book has focused throughout on discipline and routine. It has attempted to help you develop skills which will in turn help you write professionally and successfully. There has been a format, even formulae at times. All have been tested; all work. But, let's not forget to have fun.

No one can have fun in the pool if they're afraid of the water, just as no writer can have fun writing if fear is churning away inside. That's why we learn the basic skills to keep afloat, make the progress we want and see how we can push ourselves a little further each time. By now, I hope readers of this book will have lost their fear, jumped in, and experimented with the strokes which work. Now, in this final chapter, I would like to share some of the guilty secrets regular writers harbour. Sometimes they cheat a little; sometimes they invent new and weird patterns. Some work, some don't. They don't mind because they know they can always fall back on the old routines. They've lost their fear, but not their respect. They're not afraid to look silly occasionally.

Let me tell you a few stories about some of the people you've met in this book. Some have been named, others have lost their personal identities in that ultimate arrogance of the author, with their advice generalized. One who has influenced me and thousands of other writers is long dead, although her work has been reprinted for decades. Her name is Dorothea Brande and her book, *Becoming a Writer*, left me breathless when I first read it years ago. The original appeared in 1934 and was republished by Macmillan nearly 50 years later (Brande, 1983).

On becoming a writer

Written only a few decades after Freud began to publish his works on the unconscious, Brande's book is filled with concepts of unconscious and left brain/right brain behaviour that had only begun to be widely accepted. Her references to Freud and other psychoanalysts demonstrate that she was a learned and well-read woman, able to apply a fairly new science to a profession as old as writing.

Her basic assumption, and mine, is that we Westerners tend to be dominated by our conscious mind. This is our rational, analytical left brain which is self-confident, educated, logical and ruthless when it comes to anything resembling the murky non-entity it will grudgingly admit as the unconscious, the right brain – the intuition. While it might admit to it, it doesn't like it. Subject a 'gut feeling' or an intuitive thought to analysis and it will shortly conclude that the feeling has failed the benchmark of analytical thought. Having failed, it cannot exist and we are urged to dismiss it. Unfortunately, we are so well trained in rational thought that we tend to agree. We put aside our 'funny feeling' or flash of inspiration and re-apply ourselves to the tried and tested extrapolative discipline of logic.

The problem is that, sometimes, our 'funny feelings' are right. They cannot, of course, withstand the merciless scourge of the analyst, but they are no less right for that. We have all experienced it in our personal lives, but are loath to admit it in our professional lives. Interestingly, the few people who tend to admit it are often the most successful. Ask chief executives how they make decisions, and they will tell you that they base their decisions on a blend of facts and feeling. Sometimes they call intuition 'judgement' because it sounds better, but it's a 'funny feeling' all the same.

Academic rigour will fail us so long as we refuse to allow the intuitive mind to enter. The world is not composed of rights and wrongs or blacks and whites. It's awfully grey out there and just when we think we've finally nailed down a universal theory it explodes in our face. For decades we smugly said it was impossible for an object to move faster than the speed of light, but only recently it was reported that a group of scientists now think it is possible, provided we take into consideration that the universe is warped. We can't travel faster than the speed of light if we travel in a straight line, but we might be able to take a short cut. Funny what we can devise when we think outside our existing paradigms. Physicist Niels Bohr was asked which theory of light is right, particle or wave, and he answered 'both'. It depends on your point of view. Is that bad science? I think not.

Often, the most significant breakthroughs occur by 'accident'. Accident, like judgement, is a word people often find more comfortable to use than intuition. A lateral thought or a supposedly disparate set of circumstances suddenly creates an unexpected, but plausible, solution. It happens all the time, but how do we prove it? If we can't prove it, does it mean it doesn't exist?

The relevance of intuitive thought to writing is profound and unshakeable. Sometimes, by letting ourselves float around for a while after all the hard work is done, we find the next phase of writing comes more easily, or we are suddenly struck by an insight or conclusion which had previously escaped us. Such insight is the holy grail of all writers and all researchers, but how do we capture it?

Brande developed a method to train the intuitive mind to talk to us more readily. She concluded, after reading Freud and his contemporaries, that the intuitive or unconscious mind would, in most circumstances, be unwilling to converse with the rational conscious mind. Ordering it to come out into the light to reveal its secrets was a sure way to send it back into hiding. After all, it knows the score. We have been trained from childhood to dispense with such inconclusive meandering. It was fine to ask as a child 'what colour is a doggie's woof-woof?' but should we posit the question as an adolescent we would be told to stop being so silly. Our intuition learned the hard way, and no amount of lecturing it will change its mind. We have to use another method. Brande proposed trickery.

Teasing the insights

The first rule is to silence the analytical mind. When all the research is done, when the preparation is over, when the skills have been honed, we can let the rational mind have a rest. Tell it to go play chess with a computer or read *War and Peace* in the original. Brande advised letting the intuition go to work when the analytical mind is shut down. She suggested rising half an hour earlier than usual and, without talking to anyone, switching on a radio, reading a newspaper or doing anything else to excite the rational mind into wakefulness, throw yourself towards the nearest desk and paper and start to write. Just write, for 15 minutes the first day, gradually building up to half an hour. Let the words flow on to the paper from the subconscious which is not yet fully roused from its dream state. Then, most importantly, don't read it.

Write about your research, write about what interested you, write about what you feel like writing about. After a few weeks, allow yourself to read the early morning writings and see what patterns are emerging. What is that elusive right side of the brain telling you? What lateral thoughts are buried in the scrawl which you now are subjecting to analysis? What are you learning or unlearning?

Inner writing

I commend Brande's book to anyone who wants to use the power of their subconscious knowledge. She offers many more techniques and details, and following her recommended training programme is a guaranteed way to unblock intellectual freezes which your analytical mind has failed to melt.

A popular series of books, by Timothy Gallwey, developed the same theme. His *Inner Skiing* (Gallwey and Kriegel, 1991) and other 'inner' titles are based on the idea that our intellect too often takes over when it is least needed. What happens when you think about making a perfect turn on the ski slope? You fall down. What happens when you berate yourself into hitting the ball just at the proper angle? You lose your swing. The premise is that we have trained ourselves to perform well, and now we just have to let ourselves get on with it. That's when our intuition, our 'knowing' takes over.

No author can rely exclusively on his or her analytical mind. Sometimes, the knowledge that lurks deeper, gained through experience and osmosis, needs to be allowed to come out and play.

Reading for quality

Good writers are often poor at reiterating the rules of grammar. They know that a sentence doesn't sound just right, but they can't tell you why. They can, however, rewrite it until it is perfect. How have they developed that ear for what works and what doesn't? Most of them do it by reading writers better than themselves. Ask yourself what diet you are feeding to nurture your writer's brain. Escapist novels? Great plots, lousy syntax. Daily newspapers? I often recommend the world's best-selling newspaper, the British-based *Sun* to members of my groups who want to be more professional in their skills. It is surprising how so many of my academic colleagues disparage this downmarket tabloid. The *Sun* is a wonderful example of great writing because, on page 2, it distils the world news into a few paragraphs. Anyone who can summarize the situation in Bosnia or the state of the economy in 300 words deserves credit. It also reflects perfectly the tastes of its market.

But, more importantly, what great authors do you read regularly? One of the best editors I know once gave himself a break for a few weeks to brush up his writing style. On the reading list was George Orwell (*Nineteen Eighty-Four*), Evelyn Waugh (*Brideshead Revisited*), F. Scott Fitzgerald (*The Great Gatsby*) and Martin Amis (*London Fields*) – all of them masters at crafting words. We develop a feel for what is great writing by a process of osmosis. If we subject ourselves only to the mediocre, then we will mirror it.

Keeping fit

Developing writing skills is like any form of training. It takes time, patience and a regular routine to reinforce the skills. No one stands up to play at the Albert Hall having thought about it only the day before. They have practised for years, as do the great writers.

If writing well is your aspiration, then expose yourself to people who write well. Keep yourself fit by writing regularly, even if you are not currently working on a paper. The time will come when another deadline hovers on the horizon and the last thing you want is to be out of breath after the first paragraph. People who train for physical fitness are often pleasantly surprised at how quickly the body responds and gets into shape. They are equally unpleasantly surprised by how quickly their muscles turn to flab when they stop for a few weeks. Writing is like that, too. To keep it easy, to be able to turn the flow on and off at will, requires practice. Keep in shape.

Good writers don't have to wait for inspiration, they create their own. They do it through regularly communicating with both their analytical and intuitive minds and by developing the requisite skills until they are second nature. And then, they play awhile.

Developing your personal style will come, but do not make the mistake of so many new writers who think that all the rules are made to be broken. The rules are made to ease communication and only when we are confident about how they work can we bend them a little. Thousands of undergraduates try to write a stream of consciousness, but only James Joyce remains on the reading list. Thousands of painters throw oil paint at a canvas before realizing that, for all his abstract configurations, Picasso remains a technically brilliant artist whose sketches are faithful both to his subject and his art. Dylan Thomas was dismissed by some as an undisciplined drunk, but many of his poems were created entirely according to a rigorous set of rules. Structure allows us the freedom to roam within.

Readers have received much advice in this book from editors, reviewers, authors and me. I'll leave the last to a widely published academic writer, Professor Stephen Drew of McMaster University in Canada. He kindly sent me a comprehensive list of recommendations to new authors, most of which are reflected in this book. But his last line is the most important to remember: 'Take your time and don't give up. Believe in yourself.'

In the end, the analyses of our editors, reviewers and readers determine how well we communicate. That doesn't stop us from being informed by our intuition and, as we do so, to perhaps briefly inform theirs.

Appendix

Appendix

PAPER REVIEW FORM
MANAGEMENT CASES QUARTERLY

Please evaluate the paper on each of the dimensions in the following questions:

Name of Case: ....

1. Can this article be classed as a case study?   Y ☐   N ☐

2. Is the material presented in the case adequately detailed, interesting and informative?

    Y ☐   N ☐

3. Is the commentary sufficient for students to analyse and apply their skills and develop potential solutions?

    Y ☐   N ☐

4. Is it possible for students to identify what may be seen as key problem areas, major opportunities, etc.

    Y ☐   N ☐

5. Please consider the following and tick appropriately:

	Poor	Below Average	Average	Above Average	Outstanding
Problem formulation	____	____	____	____	____
Likely interest in topic	____	____	____	____	____
Organisation (logical flow, use of headings)	____	____	____	____	____
Communications (readability, grammar, clarity)	____	____	____	____	____
Conclusion and recommendations	____	____	____	____	____
Contribution to discipline	____	____	____	____	____

6. Is there an identifiable situation at the core of the case?

    Y ☐   N ☐

7. Does the case address strategic operations or tactical issues?

    Strategic   Y ☐   N ☐   *Tactical*   Y ☐   N ☐

8. Is the case capable of being used in a range of teaching situations?

                                                Y ☐   N ☐

9. Will the case appeal to a wide audience both in terms of level of study, major area
    of course, cultural and knowledge background?

                                                Y ☐   N ☐

10. Where numerical information is included in the case is its inclusion sufficiently
    rich in detail to make it possible for it to be analysed effectively?

                                                Y ☐   N ☐

11. What is your overall recommendation regarding this case study?
    Please tick

    _____ Accept

    _____ Accept with Minor Revisions (reviewer does not intend to see manuscript
          again)

    _____ Revise, Major Revisions (if properly revised, paper is publishable)

    _____ Revise, major Revisions – Risky (it is not clear that adequate revisions can be
          made, however author should be allowed to try)

    _____ Reject

12. Please provide a constructive, kind, professional set of evaluative comments
    regarding this case study (to be sent to the Author(s)):

    ● These comments should (1) explain your favourable or unfavourable reaction
       to the paper and (2) suggest possible improvements.

    ● These comments will be sent to the author(s), so they should be typed on a
       separate sheet of plain paper (no letterhead, no watermarked paper).

    ● Put the title of the paper and the paper number at the top of the sheet of
       comments.

Thank you very much for serving as a reviewer!

References

Chapter 1

Richardson, B. (1993), 'Why we probably will not save mankind: A "natural" configuration of crisis-proneness', *Disaster Prevention and Management*, **2**, (4).

Chapter 2

Bjelland, Dahl and Partners (1994), *The Keys to Breakthrough Performance*, Oslo: Performance Group.
Hague, D. (1995), *The Independent*, 30 August.
Redfern, M. (1993), 'I wannabe: the framework for continuing professional development', *Librarian Career Development*, **1**, (1).

Chapter 3

Clapp, E.J. (1994), 'Welfare and the role of women: the juvenile court movement', *Journal of American Studies*, **28** (3), pp. 359–83.
Day, A. and Peters, J. (1994), 'Quality indicators in academic publishing', *Library Review*, **45**, (3/4).
Grönroos, C. (1994), 'Relationship marketing', *Management Decision*, **33**, (2).
Kaiser, L. and De Jong, R. (1995), 'Induction of odor preference in a specialist insect parasitoid', *Animal Learning and Behaviour*, **23**, (1).

Chapter 4

Clapp, E.J. (1994) 'Welfare and the role of women: the juvenile court movement', *Journal of American Studies*, **28**, (3), pp. 359–83.

Ecker, D.J. and Crooke, S.T. (1995), 'Combinatorial drug discovery: which methods will produce the greatest value?', *Biotechnology*, **13**, April.

Lund, T., Sponheim, S.R., Iacono, W.G. and Clementz, B.A. (1995), 'Internal consistency reliability of resting EEG power spectra in schizophrenic and normal subjects', *Psychophysiology*, **32**.

Chapter 5

Duffin, M. (1995), 'On the shoulders of giants', *TQM Magazine*, **7**, (2).

Pirsig, R. (1974), *Zen and the Art of Motorcycle Maintenance*, London: Corgi.

Young, K.M. and Cooper C.L. (1995), 'Occupational stress in the ambulance service: a diagnostic study', *Journal of Managerial Psychology*, **10**, (3).

Chapter 6

Green, Y.P. and Wind, H. (1975), 'New way to measure consumers' judgements', *Harvard Business Review*, July–August.

Chapter 8

Krause, P. and Fox, J. (1994), 'An argumentation-based approach to risk assessment', *IMA Journal of Mathematics Applied in Business and Industry*, **5**, pp. 249–63.

Mitra, P.K.S. and Kundu, M.K. (1994), 'Fingerprint classification using a fuzzy multilayer perceptron', *Neural Computing and Applications*, **2**, pp. 227–33.

Chapter 10

Ansoff, H.I. (1965), *Corporate Strategy*, New York: McGraw-Hill.

Biemans, W.G. and Harmsen, H. (1995), 'Overcoming the barriers to market-oriented product development', *Journal of Marketing Practice: Applied Marketing Science*, **1**, (2).

Chapter 11

Cooter, R. (1995), 'Law and unified social theory', *Journal of Law and Society*, **22**, (1).

In Howard, K. and Sharp, J. (1983), *The Management of a Student Research Project*, Aldershot: Gower. In this work, the authors refer to the work of Monroe, Meredith and Fisher who selected typical comment patterns authors can expect their readers to make (Monroe, J., Meredith, C. and Fisher, K. (1977), *The Science of Scientific Writing*, Dubuque, Iowa: Kendall/Hurst).

Focused discussion on the subject of style in electronic 'open access' publishing has proved to be a debate topic in a number of Internet conferences. At the time of writing the following Internet sites at http://www.mcb.co.uk; theschat@timsup2.demon.co.uk and through the British Computer Society's electronic publishing specialist group meetings and seminars, http://.warwick.ac.uk cover the topic.

Chapter 12

Strunk, W. and White, E.B. (1979), *The Elements of Style*, 3rd edn, London: Macmillan.

Chapter 14

Brande, D. (1983), *Becoming a Writer*, London: Macmillan.
Gallwey, T. and Kriegel, B. (1991), *Inner Skiing*, London: Bantam Books.

Index

Coaching and Mentoring

Nigel MacLennan

The coaching/mentoring approach is probably the most effective way of helping others to achieve optimum performance in the workplace. Dr MacLennan's book covers the entire subject from basic skills to designing and implementing a tailor-made coaching and mentoring system. He starts by explaining the nature of achievement and the factors that determine it, and then introduces a seven-stage model that will enable managers and supervisors to encourage their people to develop their skills. He examines the problems commonly encountered and shows how to overcome them or, in some cases, turn them to positive account.

The book is interactive throughout, using cartoons, humour, self-assessment questions, case studies and illustrations to reinforce the text. A particularly valuable feature is a set of checklists that together summarize the key elements involved.

Coaching and Mentoring is, quite simply, a comprehensive manual of the best methods known today of helping people to succeed.

1995   ·   336 pages   0 566 07562 8

Gower

How to Organize a Conference

Iain Maitland

Next to making a presentation, organizing a conference is probably the task most likely to induce panic in even the most competent of managers. So many details to attend to! So many things to go wrong! And all of it taking place in public!

But help is at hand. Using a unique blend of questions, checklists and illustrative documents, Iain Maitland's book will guide you through the minefield. With its aid you will find yourself planning, promoting and staging a successful event - and remembering to evaluate it afterwards so that the next one will be even better.

From this book you will learn how to • set appropriate objectives • establish a sensible budget - and adhere to it • draft an appealing programme • plan a realistic schedule • choose a suitable venue • publicize the event • speak well in public • use equipment to best advantage • stage rehearsals • manage the event itself • follow through and much more besides.

The fourteen chapters cover in detail every aspect of conference organizing, and are supported by a reference section giving details of useful tools and contacts. At the end is a comprehensive checklist indexed to the text, providing both a complete summary and a way of looking back at any particular item. It may be possible to run a successful conference without Iain Maitland's book - but why take that risk?

1996   256 pages   0 566 07552 0

Gower

Professional Proposal Writing

Jane Fraser

What is the best way to structure a proposal? What style should it be written in? How can you demonstrate your capabilities to a potential client in writing? How do you distinguish your company from the competition?

These are some of the questions Jane Fraser addresses in this lively and practical guide. Based on the proposal-writing courses she runs for Oxford University, her book will help you to organize your ideas to maximum effect. She also suggests some standard formats for proposals and sales letters. Using entertaining real-life examples Dr Fraser provides simple rules for clear, reader-friendly writing and reveals the secrets of persuasive prose. Advice on layout, illustration, printing and binding is also here. Finally, she explains how to develop your proposal into a powerful presentation designed to win you new business.

The strength of a proposal can gain business or lose it. The stakes can often be high and the pressure to get it right intense. For sales and marketing people, managers, consultants, engineers and technical specialists of every kind, *Professional Proposal Writing* will be an invaluable aid to anyone who's struggled with proposals in the past or is faced with constructing them in the future.

1995   262 pages   0 566 07536 9

Gower

Professional Report Writing

Simon Mort

The ability to write reports that really convince is an invaluable management tool, yet it rarely features amongst the list of skills managers need to be effective. Simon Mort gives that skill the attention it deserves, in the most thorough book on the subject available.

As well as helpful analysis he provides practical guidance on such topics as:

- deciding the format
- structuring a report
- stylistic pitfalls and how to avoid them
- making the most of illustrations
- ensuring a consistent layout

The theme throughout is fitness for purpose, and the text is enriched by a wide variety of examples drawn from business, industry and government. The annotated bibliography includes a review of the leading dictionaries and reference books. Simon Mort's book is an indispensable reference work for managers, civil servants, local government officers, consultants and professionals of every kind.

1992   232 pages   Hardback   0 566 02712 7   Paperback   0 566 07669 1

Gower

Stand and Deliver

Ralph L Kliem and Irwin S Ludin

David Michaels is afraid. His palms sweat. His knees threaten to buckle. And his tongue, like his stomach, seems to be tied in knots. For David is due to give a series of presentations.

His objective is to win support for his project to save sick children in Amazonia. Fortunately, help is at hand in the unlikely shape of Demosthenes, the 4th century BC Greek orator. Under his tutelage David overcomes his fears and learns how to create a powerful presentation. What he learns, he realises, can be applied to any presentation, large or small.

By following David as he gradually masters the techniques involved you will learn how to:
• define the audience • determine what to say
• organize the content • control nervousness
• deliver in style • use visual aids
• deal with questions.

The fictional treatment makes this an entertaining as well as an informative guide. As an additional aid to learning the key points are summarized in checklist form at the end of the book. *Stand and Deliver* will be valued by all managers faced with the need to give effective presentations.

1995   286 pages   0 566 07574 1

Gower